Franz Rosenzweig's "The New Thinking"

Library of Jewish Philosophy

Franz Rosenzweig's

"The New Thinking"

Edited and Translated from the German by
Alan Udoff *and* Barbara E. Galli

Syracuse University Press

Copyright © 1999 by Syracuse University Press
Syracuse, New York 13244-5160
All Rights Reserved

First Edition 1999
99　00　01　02　03　04　　6　5　4　3　2　1

The paper used in this publication meets the minimum requirements of
American National Standard for Information Sciences—Permanence of Paper
for Printed Library Materials, ANSI Z39.48-1984 ∞™

Library of Congress Cataloging-in-Publication Data
Rosenzweig, Franz, 1886–1929.
[Neue Denken. English]
Franz Rosenzweig's "The new thinking" / edited and translated by
Alan Udoff and Barbara E. Galli.
p.　cm.—(Library of Jewish philosophy)
Includes bibliographical references and index.
ISBN 0-8156-2783-1 (cloth: alk. paper). — ISBN 0-8156-2784-X
(paper: alk. paper)
1. Rosenzweig, Franz, 1886–1929. Stern der Erlösung.　2. Judaism.
3. Philosophy, Jewish.　I. Udoff, Alan, 1943–　.　II. Galli,
Barbara E. (Barbara Ellen), 1949–　.　III. Title.　IV. Series.
BM565.R5913　1998
296.3—dc21　98-22126

Manufactured in the United States of America

Contents

Acknowledgments

The authors wish to acknowledge with gratitude the generosities without which this work could not have been realized. Rainer Nägele, Anna and Horace Rosenberg, Willi Schmidt, and Dana Hollander devoted their time and contributed their knowledge to the translation throughout its many revisions. Much of its accuracy and elegance derives from their efforts. Diane Spielman (Leo Baeck Institute) assisted in the researching of archival materials. Elaine Lustig Cohen kindly gave permission to reprint Joachim Neugroschel's translation of Margarete Susman's review of *The Star of Redemption,* from Arthur A. Cohen's *The Jew: Essays from Martin Buber's Journal,* Der Jude, *1916–1928.* Sidney Breitbart supported this undertaking both materially and personally. Finally, The Louis L. Kaplan Chair of Baltimore Hebrew University substantially assisted with the funding of the research for this volume.

Alan Udoff is Louis L. Kaplan Professor of Philosophy at Baltimore Hebrew University. He is editor of *Kafka and the Contemporary Critical Performance: Centenary Readings* and *Leo Strauss's Thought: Toward a Critical Engagement*.

Barbara E. Galli is Aaron Aaronov Chair of Judaic Studies at the University of Alabama. She is author of *Franz Rosenzweig and Jehuda Halevi: Translating, Translation, and Translators*.

Franz Rosenzweig's "The New Thinking"

1

"The New Thinking"
An Introduction

BARBARA E. GALLI

There is no escape from this book. It will call in all hiding places of reason and non-reason; it itself will disappear, but it will have moved humanity, and Judaism will be named after it.

—Rudolf Hallo
Führerblatt des J. W.-B. Kameraden

Cautionary Remarks

Franz Rosenzweig intended his supplementary essay to *The Star of Redemption* to speak to a specific audience: those who had read the *Star* between the year of its appearance, 1921, and 1924. More narrowly, the essay is addressed only to those, among these first readers, who had had difficulty with the book.[1] Granted, this was nearly everyone; and it is questionable whether we today have less difficulty with it than the first readers. Nevertheless, according to instructions that Rosenzweig sets into the essay itself, "The New Thinking" was not to be published in any subsequent edition of the *Star*. Composed for this specific audience, then, "The New Thinking" appeared in the October 1925 issue of *Der Morgen*.[2]

Are we justified in reading the essay as readers of the *Star*, or must we confine ourselves at most to reading "The New Thinking" as readers of a historical piece that records a private conversation of others and that we therefore approach only as interested scholars—or eavesdroppers? *Qua* historical piece with an explicitly specified audience in the history of modern Jewish and philosophical thought, is "The New Thinking" bound exclusively to that first audience and therefore not relevant to our reading of the *Star*? Perhaps this might have been so under circumstances other than the ones that did ensue.

Before either *The Star of Redemption* or its explanatory essay "The New Thinking" could take firm hold in Jewish thought or in philosophic thought generally, let alone have any moving effect much beyond the inner circle that was already practicing or developing the new thinking anyway, the realm of Nazism entered the world.

The "new thinking" began to receive sustained attention only since the early seventies in America, and since the eighties in Europe and Israel. Even now this attention is restricted to a relatively small number of scholars. Thus, reaching a definitive answer as to our place as readers of "The New Thinking" would be an elusive endeavor. The best clues for an adequate answer would be found in what Rosenzweig perceived as troubling to those early readers, and to find these clues, we need to read "The New Thinking." Perhaps we may even consider ourselves to be early readers. Let us see.

These first readers had expressed, in various explicit and implicit ways, as have almost all subsequent readers, some of their difficulties with the profoundly complex religio-philosophical book. The kind, degree, and extent of the readers' problems covered a great range. Some of the more earnest readers, aware that they did not understand exactly what was involved in Rosenzweig's "complete renewal in philosophical thinking" (*NT,* 69), could still not pinpoint precisely what they did not understand. These readers, therefore, misunderstood certain of the *Star*'s features that hinged on these unperceived pivotal points. Clouds of clinging preconceptions from the "old thinking" precluded lucid reading by others. These readers still inhabited, as if it were the only viable house for thought, the edifice of enquiry into essences, into being. Still others were happier to own than to read the book and, despite ignorance of the contents of their possession, to participate in discussions of the *Star.* These last readers erroneously presumed that the pages unread by them were replete with a modern reiteration of Jewish religious feeling, coupled with a concern to call out to young German Jews and to welcome them back to their heritage.

Within this group of early readers, there were, as well, a small number of readers who "could have written the book just as well or better than" the author (*NT,* 68). Rosenzweig is referring here to several other thinkers of the time, some in his own circle, who were also passionately concerned, in the wake of World War I, with the development of new philosophical thinking, and who also related their questions closely to notions of the vitality of speech and language. The essay is not addressed to these few. Importantly, however, among them a conversation about "The New Thinking" had already begun, and it continued in arenas such as the Patmos Circle, and the circle's periodical *Die Kreatur*.[3]

All those who had received the *Star* not only incited Rosenzweig in one fashion or another to write the essay, but, through their specific reception, provided Rosenzweig with the cues as to what areas he should emphasize, correct, or redirect.

A few weeks after writing "The New Thinking," Rosenzweig told his cousin, Hans Ehrenberg, in a letter dated 11 March 1925, that

> a printed essay can only take into account the six hundred Jews who own the Star of Redemption (there may be a hundred copies among the others). In Jewish circles the book has become downright famous. I could show you the most amazing comments. This prestige really gives me my only platform, for I am writing *against* this prestige. Of course not against the quantity of it, which pleases me well enough, but against its quality. For this reason I deliberately exaggerate in the other direction, the general philosophical. . . . [The *Star*] has made me famous among the Jews but has not obstructed my influence with the Jews. And the reason for both is that they haven't read it. Again and again I am amazed at how little its readers know it. Everybody thinks it is an admonition to eat kosher. The beautiful phrase of my Catholic name-saint: *tantum quisque intelligit, quantum operatur,* applies also to the passive *intelligitur.* And this is all to the good.[4]

The early readers of whom Rosenzweig writes to his cousin had, to Rosenzweig's distress, one-sidedly and narrowly presumed there to be a preaching of a return to Judaism in the *Star*.[5] Whereas the *Star*, on philosophical grounds, affirms Judaism as a tenable theological *and* philosophical worldview that can successfully be lived in time, it affirms the same for Christianity. Yet neither is affirmed as final or total truths, or realities. The ultimate truth is beyond both, after the fulfillment of time. Thus, whereas the *Star*'s title page designates the work as a "Jewish book," apologetics, polemics, or homiletics on behalf of Judaism were hardly its prime or basic intention.[6] By weighting in the essay the philosophical inclinations of the book, and by elaborating upon its philosophical method, Rosenzweig attempts to correct the imbalance in its reception. Had the reception caught hold of only the purely philosophical in the book, Rosenzweig would likely have weighted the essay theologically, or, perhaps, not written it at all.

In his naming it a Jewish book, Rosenzweig means that he wrote it as a Jewish man of flesh and blood though at the same time as a philosopher: he wrote not from the bloodless point of view of detached, "objective" reason, that is, not only out of the "discipline" of philosophy, but as a human being who philosophizes. Although he does not want to conceal that he is a committed, believing Jew, the disclosure of his Jewishness appears in his modes of expression and biblical references rather than in any explicit statement. He writes not so much "about" Judaism as he writes philosophy Jewishly: with Jewishly verbal frames of reference. This, Rosenzweig wants to emphasize, is an aspect of the "new thinking," that is, to philosophize as a particular person, with first and last name: Franz Rosenzweig. As such he is therefore not professing, teaching, or promoting religion *per se,* Judaism or any other, in the *Star.* In this connection, he affirms, to some extent, the "point-of-view philosopher," the philosopher who is self-consciously a particular human being during the philosophizing process.[7] The point at which Rosenzweig cautions against following Schopenhauer,

Nietzsche, and Kierkegaard is where privatization might enter: isolated philosophizing in the name of non-relating self.

Without once using the term "religion," as Rosenzweig points out in the essay, the discussion in the *Star,* instead, speaks of religions as "forms." These forms are various attempts at expressing and enacting reality, some based on a claim of divine revelation, some not. Rosenzweig the philosopher is interested in the extent to which these forms accurately express and enact truths.

Philosophically, Rosenzweig describes Judaism and Christianity as being most representative of human enactments and embodiments of truth. He means that these are embodied as temporal forms that aim at enacting a perception of Truth, or at establishing eternity in time. He does not mean that the individual Jew or individual Christian is, by virtue of being Christian or Jewish, any closer to God, or vice versa, than, say, an individual pagan of ancient Greece.[8] But these two "forms" express, to Rosenzweig, in their respective liturgical calendars, more accurately than any other "form," how things actually are, and actually happen, in the world. Also, both these forms as theological sensibilities insist on what is prior to and posterior to creation as real beginning and real ending of the world. It is only, then, between the beginning and ending of the world—that entire stretch between creation and redemption: revelation—that their forms may be given a chance for performance. This is one reason why a "new thinker," or "speech-thinker,"[9] might most easily make sense of and move into the New Thinking out of Jewish or Christian frames of reference. Speech-thinking, however, is not perceived by Rosenzweig as being unique to the Christian or Jew. It is not so much a matter of particular persons as it is a matter of "forms" that nourish a person's way of thinking and living and of viewing the world. Christianity and Judaism as "forms" are conducive to the "new thinking," but the Christian or Jew whose nourishment, theologically and philosophically, stems from the dominant influences "from Ionia to Jena" will still experience the shock of the "newness" of Rosenzweig's method.

Poets, Rosenzweig notices, have always understood this way of thinking. Among the host of philosophers in the Western tradition, therefore, only those who possess strong poetic affinities incline toward the borders of the "new thinking." The medieval philosopher and poet, Jehuda Halevi (before 1075–1141), counts among these, whereas the "unpoetic" Maimonides, who inclines toward the Aristotelian method, does not. From the Romantic period, Johann Georg Hamann (1730–1788), who firmly maintained that speech is sacred, and who was admired by Rosenzweig,[10] perhaps through the influence of Eugen Rosenstock-Huessy, embodies par excellence a philosopher with a poetic leaning.[11]

The problems that Rosenzweig addresses in "The New Thinking" show both how the "old thinking" is entwined with and basic to the new, and to what extent, in what ways, and why the new thinking arises out of and unravels itself from the old. The inherent problems of the old, which the new now wants to leave behind, lie chiefly in the questions asked by philosophers, and philosophy itself as it had come to be known and done for two thousand years.

In a concrete sense, this interdependence of philosophical and Jewish ingredients which Rosenzweig puts into the *Star* characterizes a chief principle of the "new thinking": one does philosophy, or science, in a way that is not disengaged from one's life as lived, that is not disengaged from one's theoretical beliefs. Each ingredient—philosophy and religious belief—retains its distinctive flavor. Philosophy and theology remain separate, independent *fields* of enquiry, but a philosopher and a theologian live in the same person. Yet, when tried together, as neither mixture nor blend, but as raspberries and cream, each lends a new taste to the other. For the new thinking, each becomes unnourishing on its own, and eventually results in starvation. Belief, as it overarches, reaches down, and takes root in one's life, forbids a walled separation between faith and "reason."[12] The human being needs both.[13]

"The New Thinking" as a Guide for Reading the *Star*

The essay is explicitly not to be made into an introduction to the *Star* for future readers, and yet Rosenzweig's instructions go against the grain both of human nature and of historical circumstances. Rosenzweig's own death at an early age, followed soon after by the loss of most of German Jewry under Nazism, together resulted in a hiatus of readership for the *Star*. Rosenzweig studies have been sparse, sporadic, and slow to take firm root in soil outside Germany for transplanted growth. Today, Rosenzweig's thought is given very little notice in Germany, where he is known almost solely for his collaborative work with Buber on Bible translation. The translation into English on American soil thirty years ago, and into French on France's soil twenty years ago, have brought new life to the work. The Israeli reception has varied widely.

Still, the *Star of Redemption* is dense, often gnomic, and always dauntingly brilliant. The little essay "The New Thinking" is more readable by contrast, and reads as if it were a guide to labyrinthine lines of thought. There does not seem to be any real wrong in this, even with Rosenzweig's directive. To enter by a side door does not mean for sure we will not arrive at a good understanding of the fullness of the shifting patterns of the construction of an edifice. At the same time, if we do gain a favorable understanding of the edifice with this introduction to it, we will wish to return, to enter by the main gate, and to experience the details in their intended order of experience and understanding.

Hans Trüb, who had read the essay but had not yet read the *Star*, is one example of a person who entered the *Star* through "The New Thinking." He wrote to Martin Buber on 31 August 1926:

> I recently read Franz Rosenzweig's essay "The New Thinking" in *Der Morgen*. [. . .] One derives an exceedingly compelling inspiration from him and his position. I am looking forward to reading his *Star of Redemption* soon. [. . .] I can see Rosenzweig before me in the flesh, immured in his paralyzed body: the highest measure of disability for a person still to turn toward this world. Rosenzweig does not turn away from it. . . . Does it not show us how all of us, placed into this world and attached to it, endure our being sent away from it? Must not the world, the Creation, be redeemed at some temporal point after all? [. . .] I love Rosenzweig because of the cross he bears. He will always be a force for good in my life.[14]

Certainly there are benefits from the essay's pointers and emphatic directives for an illuminated reading of the *Star*. Still, to depend on the essay for an initial acquaintance with the *Star* might for some be rather like being escorted by a guide in an art gallery who lingers at only those paintings and features in those paintings which her last group had specially asked about or had displayed ignorance of. Whether the essay is read by us before or after reading the *Star,* or even for assistance while reading it, it is important to remember that we are not the essay's intended audience. In following "The New Thinking's" signposts, we are directed only in airlift fashion, touching down now and then, here and there, at this and that highlight of the terrain, and in between landings layers of clouds obstruct the view. Perhaps, after all, as for many a great work, it is best to read the *Star,* unobstructed by any criticism, or teaching, of it—the author's or anyone else's. Yet, if a great work can only serve more and more people through other avenues than the direct one, then these avenues are not merely justified, they are to be kept in good repair. Rashi is an example, and Oral Torah.

"The New Thinking," however, will approach only those depths and heights that have been excised from the *Star* for a close view; some doors will not be opened at all. "The New Thinking" is not a base upon which a full discussion of the *Star,* if unread, can be built. "In this whole essay," Rosenzweig states, "I am giving the reader of the book only pointers. If he wants to know what is in it, then he must read it. I cannot spare him that" (*NT,* 76).

Two counts make "The New Thinking" an invaluable piece. It provides us with cues not offered in the book by its leading statements and hints about the *Star*'s background *and* future, as well as by its extensive remarks about the method used. In the *Star* itself, Rosenzweig presents no direct explanation of the method. He dives into the primordial waters and begins to philosophize as a speech-thinker, or more accurately, as a storyteller. Such a lack of demonstration, especially of a "new" method, is bound to confuse some, if not most readers. Later, Rosenzweig again experienced this problem of being misunderstood in another context but for similar reasons. Nahum N. Glatzer, a student of Rosenzweig's and a member of the Freies Jüdische Lehrhaus while it was under Rosenzweig's directorship, writes the following of his teaching:

> Rosenzweig's own lecture course, attended by about one hundred persons, was a failure. He was motivated by a passionate urge to teach, to interpret, to clarify. But he was simply unable to realize the intellectual limitations of even intelligent, university-trained men and women. He did not talk their language and they did not understand his. His listeners sensed his greatness; yet he did not want to be admired, but understood. There was something tragic in the situation of a man who so fully believed in the power of the dialogue and the discussion to be doomed to a monological, one-sided activity. Thus, his direct and immediate influence extended to a small group of men and women; only indirectly, through intermediaries, through his explanatory essay, and finally, through the example of his life, did his word reach wider circles.[15]

The Star of Redemption's Integrity

The *Star* is the sort of book which resists summarization. Rosenzweig's advice in "The New Thinking" is, upon reading the essay, to read the *Star* once again. All who have tried to summarize the *Star*, as distinguished from those (including the author himself) who have sought to highlight certain features of it, blur or misrepresent that system of philosophy, often in serious ways. Gershom Scholem, for example,[16] read him as problematic with regard to mysticism and mystical concepts.[17]

However the book is read, this is clear: Rosenzweig plainly intends the *Star* to be, quite literally, read through. The book is to be undergone, experienced. This is not merely because it features a real beginning, middle, and end, but because it explicitly also has a beyond. Thus, the reader, having read through the book, actually arrives somewhere. He is at a new place. This region is not merely the fixed place called "the end of the book." The person who has read the book now has a book behind him. This "behind" is not behind in the sense of the book being "left behind," but precisely the opposite. It is behind in the sense of the most solid of tenses. The book is now embodied in the past experience of the reader, and it is encumbent upon him that the past, now fixed, be—in the person's warm, breathing being—melted into the flow of life.

The *Star*'s mandate differs from other systems' mandates. Rosenzweig says: Take my view, look around for yourself, then refute it or verify it out of your own life's experiences and those of others—not by returning to the book's pages but by drawing what is on the pages out into the days and nights of life. Thus, the one who has gone through and now carries forward the contents must move beyond the book's gateway out into what Rosenzweig calls "no-longer-book," and live. Going through the book has meant for the reader to have gone through, only theoretically perhaps, but at best, experientially in those moments lived and reflected upon between reading sessions, at worst only imaginatively, all the tenses of world time, from creation, through revelation, into redemption.

The time now lived, resumed, by the reader of the *Star* will entail a life that self-consciously lives in time stretched between creation and redemption, and in relation to the other, world, and God. All knowing, all doing will henceforth panoramically sustain their revelatory preview of all-time, the closure, the completion of time promised in creation, realized in redemption. All knowing and doing will have a "memory" of when there was nothing, and no time. All knowing and doing will yet be experienced from the individual person's particular standpoint, in a relationship with world and God, and in a temporal framework of creation-revelation-redemption.

The notion of "no-longer-book" is consonant with Rosenzweig's antitotalizing, or nonreductionist, system. The Final Day alone totalizes the multiplicities of the everydays. Only the end of a life creates the whole of that life. Only the end of the world is its fulfillment. The reader is to go on in his own, with his own life. In its respect for the individual human as an irreducible element of reality, who, moreover, has his own voice, the "new thinking" nonetheless presupposes, and desires, the effect of others' voices upon one's own. By going through the book and coming out of it, one carries another individual's comprehensive view of life, of God, world, and human being. This comprehensive view arises out of and into a tradition, both a theological one and a philosophical one.

Even if a person does not accept or internalize this view for his own subsequent behavior, attitude, or actions, or agree with it in all its details, each close reader of the *Star* cannot help but sense that it is written from the point of view of a healthy human being who writes as a man who affirms life and lifefulness. If to nothing else, one responds to Rosenzweig's wholesomeness as a thinker.[18] Even if one is not attracted to his thinking, still one is compelled to respond reflectively, beyond the book, to what he has said. One is compelled, for instance, to remember Rosenzweig's notions about full word being word *and* response in one's dealings with others "beyond the book."[19]

If Rosenzweig's *Star* is philosophically revolutionary in any way, it is so in the way that his contemporary, Gustav Landauer, defined, in political terms, revolution. "The ultimate ground of revolution, according to Landauer, is the spiritual regeneration of the individual, and concomitantly, of the moral quality of the relations between man and man. Revolution, hence, must proceed from the individual, in a personal decision of the individual to call upon and cultivate the powers of vitality and love that slumber within himself and others."[20]

Rosenzweig holds adamantly that the commandment to love one's neighbor cannot be obeyed in "loving all the world," but in loving the nearest neighbors, one by one. When he wrote to his (Christian) cousin Rudolf Ehrenberg that lengthy letter which he subsequently termed the "germ cell" [*Urzelle*] of the *Star*, Rosenzweig juxtaposes in stark opposition the "old" and the "new" thinking's notions of love of neighbor. The "old" thinking, concerned with essences, considers "the" human being as a static entity. All "relationships" are third person. The individual with first and last name is reduced to "the" human being. In the "new" thinking, the human being is only fully human once the soul is awakened by God in revelation. Authentic relationships take place under the framework of Creation, Revelation, and Redemption, that is, in time that has a direction, and a beginning and an end. He writes:

Instead of these easily and cheaply found brothers everywhere, to whom he stands in "relationship," the human has in the "connection" . . . only *himself* as his own likeness; the word of neighborly love, there a well-tempered matter of course, here becomes a voice of trumpets, for it is not said to the human in whose breast's purity surges an aspiration for voluntary *submission,* but to the deaf I, buried in its own I-ness, to this I, about which nothing can be presupposed except this, that it loves *itself.* But that is why, *after* this word [of revelation, of God's love, and of his love commandments] has opened up the deaf ear, the human now recognizes in the neighbor now really the one who is like him, recognizes him not merely as B_2, B_3, and so on, as co-inhabitant of the same world, comember of the great equation A=B, of which he after all knows only that which he *sees,*—for he recognizes him only as It, only as his brother in the forest and grove in rock and water; rather I recognize that he *is not He She It, but rather an I,* an I like I am, not a co-inhabitant of the same directionless and centerless space, not a travel acquaintance on the trip through time without beginning and end, but my brother, the consorts of my destiny, for whom "things are" exactly as for me, who also sees only one track before him as I do; my brother not in the world, in woods, and grove, in bush and water, but in the Lord.[21]

The philosophizing that takes place in the book, says Rosenzweig, is what everyone should do some time: "look around from his own stand- and life-point. But this look is not an end in itself."

> The book is not a goal which has been reached, not even a temporary one. One must be responsible for it instead of carrying itself or being carried by others of its kind. This responsibility happens in everyday [Alltag] life. Only in order to recognize and to live the day as every-day [All-tag], the day of the life of the All [All] had to be traversed. (*NT,* 100)

Reading the book can be likened to listening to a great symphony for the first time. Most of the major themes and motifs are introduced near the beginning, as a base text. One awaits their return, again and again, but not knowing in advance precisely the ways they will be played out, nor how the themes and motifs will be resolved in the end. No theme's return is repetitive; descants occur. Moreover, there will be met unrepeated melodies or even new themes along the way that are yet necessary to the whole piece. To listen to one movement only may be a worthwhile and enjoyable experience; but one cannot thereby claim to have experienced, to have understood the whole. Such is the construction of the *Star.* Themes are built up throughout the work. The birth and life and immortality of the soul, for example, is a story told that not only is threaded but unravels throughout the three parts. Death is a theme throughout. Explicit influences from Jewish mystical traditions are repeatedly in evidence. Theories of art and discussions of Eastern philosophies and religions are but two more examples of what is skillfully and smoothly woven into the rich fabric of the whole.[22] And, as in the best musical compositions, not one note is superfluous; indeed, each, upon reflection, resonates more meaningfully beside the other notes. Each phrase can be tirelessly—and with deeper appreciation each time—replayed to one's ear, now expectant, but heard as if for the first time.

Thus Rosenzweig understates the case for his book when he writes: "If he wants to know what is in it, then he must read it."

The experience of reading the *Star* is also very like, and in this case, is meant to be like, the experience of listening to a story. One can summarize a story, but ultimately only with as much success, effect, feeling, or meaning as through a summary of a poem. Stories and poems, to be what they are, or to be relived, can be told only in their (re)telling. In "The New Thinking" Rosenzweig notes that Schelling had "predicted a storytelling philosophy in the foreword of his brilliant fragment 'The Ages of the World,'" and states that part 2 of the *Star* is an attempt to fulfill this prediction. (*NT,* 81) It could be claimed that part 1 is the "once upon a time," part 2 is the story proper, and part 3 is the "(blissfully) ever after." Rosenzweig's ultimate aim is not to define or discover what the world is, but to tell the story of the world. In this storytelling connection, he describes the three parts of the *Star:* "And now this great world-poem is retold in three tenses. Actually told only in the first, the book of the past. In the present the story yields to the immediate exchange of speech, for of those who are present, be they human beings or God, one cannot speak in the third person, they can only be heard and addressed. And in the book of the future the language of the chorus reigns, for even the individual grasps the future only where and when he can say We" (*NT,* 85–86).

If a story is a good one, every event and every character's entry and exit and action take place how and where they do for a reason or reasons. The reason becomes evident at the end, but the route to the end is at least as important as the end itself. This is true of a good story, of the Bible, of Rosenzweig's book, and of his speech-thinking philosophy. The understanding, in all four, happens *as* the story moves along its course.

The world story, because story, has of course moved on since 1925. With this movement, the story of Rosenzweig's book also changes, as if the original becomes in some senses more alive now than it had been in 1920. Still, as vibrant and audible as the *Star* might now have become through the vocality of English, Israeli, and French language spirits and the power of scholarship, it is *also* a book of 1920, written during the excruciating turbulence and spiritually and intellectually numbing shock of World War I. The *Star's* speech, frozen now as book, melts also in new rivers of readerships, with end-of-the-century viewpoints. If, as Hans Ehrenberg claims in his review, the *Star* is written from the viewpoint of being a war book, then at the end of this century our points of view are sadly compounded and more complex.

When Is the Timely Time for the *Star?*

The apparently, or actually, unfathomable events in every arena that are occurring with equally seemingly or actually unfathomable speed in *today's* world do not themselves, however, adequately bear the reasons for the current, first truly widespread interest in the *Star.* In "The New Thinking," as in the *Star,* Rosenzweig marks 1800, that is to say Hegel, as the culmination and perfection of the philosophical enquiry undertaken by Idealism, and therefore as its death. That this death was not properly mourned by respectfully leaving it behind and turning to refreshing life-forms, but was instead spectrally carried forward, incited Rosenzweig, himself a great and devoted student of Hegel,[23] to initiate the "new" thinking. The "old," having lived a long and truly fruitful life, had now died in rich maturity. World War I, to Rosenzweig, was the tragic but inevitable suicidal result of dragging along in philosophy the now longtime lifeless carcass of the idealist inquiry. Instead of burying Idealism, that grand two-thousand-year long enquiry into essences, allowing a monument to be erected to its success and permitting its reposeful decay to fertilize new life, post-Hegelianism choked in dank airlessness and rootlessness beneath the earth. For over one hundred years, the death of Idealism had been denied.

The pains arising from philosophy's stifled enclosure in the history of philosophy, from the loss of the Enlightenment's dreams, which had had their appropriate time in the world story, from the death of the autonomy of reason, and finally from each individual death eventuated by World War I, all came to be embedded on multiple levels in philosophers' psyches. What sense was left? How was meaning to be determined? The primary tool, reason, had broken down. What tool was now to be trusted?

Post-Hegelians tried to numb the pain intellectually and spiritually, and to suppress it so that these multiple agonies could be borne, so that philosophy could still be done in the now old-fashioned, ineffective, redundant way, so that *Philosophia* could be believed to be still alive. Instead of being entirely numbed, these pains made themselves felt in resultant deformities of a now warped discipline. A form that had become only a shell was handled in all its fragility. In this shell's chambers bloodless, fleshless phantoms could and did hollowly echo.

As a philosophical work, as theory, as comprehensive story of the world, the *Star* stands its ground. Rosenzweig stood by it for the time that remained to him after he wrote it. And he thought it warranted a future: he requested that it be translated into Hebrew after his death. On 10 April 1923 he wrote to Buber: "May God grant that the one who undertakes the translation also knows German. In the manner of Hölderlin [*Hölderlinisch*], I mean, of course."[24] What changed for Rosenzweig himself in respect of his own system was only his "relationship to his theory." He wanted to realize it in real life. On 9 June 1924 Rosenzweig wrote to his cousin Gertrud Oppenheim, who had detected in his Halevi book something more of Rosenzweig's own voice than she had heard in the *Star:* "Nothing has changed with regard to the theory of Judaism in the *Star,* but only with regard to my relationship to this theory. Precisely if, unlike the Idealists, one fundamentally expects that the theory will be reached in practice, one must be all the more wary that one does not allow it to become the refuge of one's own indolence. This danger for sure lies in this theory."[25]

Rosenzweig, for all his desire, and success, in his personally practiced realization of his philosophy in life, has been rejected on a grave count.[26] Rosenzweig's notion that Jews live as a metahistorical people, although it was a pre-Holocaust, and pre-1948 conception, presents real problems. Great exception to this notion has been taken by many post-Holocaust thinkers.[27] Many Jews who might otherwise have held Rosenzweig in high, even proud, esteem have remained aloof from him for this reason, a reaction undoubtedly caused by a misunderstanding of his meaning of the term "metahistorical."

A clarification of Rosenzweig's intended meaning of metahistorical lies in the term "meta," meaning "beyond," but not necessarily only in a detaching sense either spatially or temporally. It can mean "not now," "not yet," "beyond this present time," while yet being fully attached to the present space and time. If so meant, then the attachment of the term "meta" to another term already denotes both a present and a future. One of the reasons for Rosenzweig's great admiration of Hermann Cohen was precisely along these lines: that the urgent moral and ethical matters of the present were not to be put off lazily to an infinite eternity, but were to be actively striven for in the concrete world now. When Rosenzweig designates man's essence as meta-ethical, he does not mean man is not to take part in ethical behavior. God, as metaphysical, does not mean he does not take part in the material world.

The misreading of Rosenzweig's term "meta" stems from a whole people's recent wounds from the Holocaust. Rosenzweig is not the only one among fellow Jews who lived just prior to but not until the Holocaust's eruption; he is not the only one who "could not have known," and seems to those who "do know" to be a misguided thinker. The judgment of those who do know perhaps in part constitutes an attempt to soothe the searing wounds cutting and cutting the body and soul of the Jewish people, an attempt to fight back against what appeared to be in hindsight a self-deceiving group of the people who stayed in the spaces where the Holocaust spread and prevailed, a group who could have left, a group now dead.

A faulty understanding of Rosenzweig's work and the ensuing rejection of it were in part the reason for the dearth of a readership for Rosenzweig and for a lacuna in scholarship. The lacuna is not important. It may have been necessary. Rosenzweig was a crucially important voice immediately after World War I, but was not helpful in the first decades after the World War II. The healing from the hurt, the ways to form the memory, the building forward: these have been more important endeavors for the past half century. They continue to be so, and yet now the lacuna may be closed for other reasons.

Rosenzweig's own life testifies to the fact that he wholeheartedly believed in Jewish action and activity in history. The Jew, however, in his *baruch ata*,[28] is already with God, needs no intermediary, and with every Shabbat, with every Yom Kippur gathers into his soul a deeper understanding, by repeated rehearsals, of redemption. The that-worldly *and* the this-worldly coincide easily in the Jew's view of life and way of living.[29] Paul Mendes-Flohr points out:

> To achieve its pristine goal of creating an *ökumene*—a world community bound in spirit and peace—history requires divine assistance. Specifically, as he argued in his theological opus, *The Star of Redemption* (1920), history caught in the quagmire of the nation-state and war can only transcend itself by being constantly prodded by a metahistorical reference that concretely embodies in the *here and now* the eschatological goal of history. Rosenzweig assigned this task of eschatological admonisher to Judaism, or rather to the Synagogue. While the nations of the world stride through history—politics and war—

as indeed they must, the Synagogue stands beyond history, that is, beyond political nationhood and enjoys an inner peace that anticipates the future promise to all peoples.[30]

Not the Jew as human being, not to Juda-ism, but to the synagogue. Rosenzweig, as evidenced in part 3 of the *Star,* describes the synagogue as the place where eternity *is* experienced, where all meet at one point: not yet *in* God, but for now in giving thanks *to* God.[31] Here it is not the static locative case for God, but the dynamic dative case, the case used for relationship. The *in*-history means, for the Christian, that he must missionize, evangelize, spread the Gospel. The world *sees the end,* is transformed by virtue of the Christian's missionary activity. The world *remains* because of the Jew. Whereas Rosenzweig perceives the Jew as already living beyond history in respect of his synagogue life, never, as stressed above, does Rosenzweig suggest that Jews be relegated to the margin to be cast outside the bounds of the fluctuation of daily commerce of human beings. On the contrary, it was Rosenzweig who first saw real possibilities for genuine dialogue, advocating

frank, open confrontation based on the real theological and existential issues that separate Jew and Christian. Rosenzweig clearly would have preferred the medieval *disputatio* to the superficial civility and the indirect manner of theological encounter of the bourgeoisie. The indirect, "academic" discourse invariably led to the distortions Rosenzweig characterized as "apologetic thinking"—the tendency to view one's "adversary" through the prism of abstract theoretical constructs . . .[32]

Further, Rosenzweig clearly advocated and saw to it through his *Lehrhaus* work that many an assimilated Jew learn to take his visible place and stand as Jew, very much in the world, and not beyond it.

When on 1 August 1920 Rosenzweig became the *Lehrhaus's* founding and innovative head, he fully understood that the time was not ripe for Jewish Studies Departments in universities. And there is no evidence that Rosenzweig thought there could be (or foresaw) a time when that day would arrive, or that he saw any particular practicality in pushing things in that direction. At the end of this same summer, he turned down a university lectureship in history at Leipzig. To accept the post would mean to dichotomize himself between privately practiced belief and public office. Rosenzweig discovered he was not capable of doing this. To his former professor, Friedrich Meinecke, who had offered him the position, Rosenzweig wrote a letter attempting an explanation for his refusal. This was on 30 August 1920, seven years after Rosenzweig's Yom Kippur experience, the day that showed to him that his intended path toward baptism was no longer necessary. The Jew, Rosenzweig learned that day, is already with God. This "metahistorical" category, however, is clearly one that brought Rosenzweig (and other "peripheral" Jews) more into than out of the world. What he calls his "dark drive," "the ghost," his "Judaism," is utterly fleshly in its rejuvenated spirituality:

> In 1913 something happened to me for which *collapse* is the only fitting name. I suddenly found myself on a heap of wreckage, or rather I realized that the road I was then pursuing was flanked by unrealities. . . . The study of history would only

have served to feed my hunger for forms, my insatiable receptivity; history to me was a purveyor of forms, no more. No wonder I inspired horror in others as well as in myself! [. . .] The one thing I wish to make clear is that scholarship no longer holds the center of my attention, and that my life has fallen under the rule of a "dark drive" which I'm aware that I merely *name* by calling it "my Judaism." The scholarly aspect of this whole process—the conversion of the historian into a philosopher—is only a corollary, though it has furnished me with a welcome corroboration of my own conviction that the "ghost I saw" was not the devil; it seems to me that I am today more firmly rooted in the earth than I was seven years ago. The man who wrote the *Star of Redemption* . . . is of a very different caliber from the author of *Hegel and the State*. Yet when all is said and done, the new book is only—a book.[33]

The Effect of the *Star* on Both Reader and Author

Out of the book's Gate, Rosenzweig, too, entered into the "no-longer-book." The letter to Meinecke is many pages in length, and more of it is worth quoting, because it explains an aspect of the "new thinking" with specific regard to this region "beyond book," where the knowledge derived from it is carried within, yet flexibly lived and applied in conversation with flesh-and-blood others:

Cognition is autonomous; it refuses to have any *answers* foisted on it from the outside. Yet it suffers without protest having certain *questions* prescribed to it from the outside (and it is here that my heresy regarding the unwritten law of the university originates). Not every question seems to me worth asking.

Scientific curiosity and omnivorous aesthetic appetite mean equally little to me today, though I was once under the spell of both, particularly the latter. Now I only inquire when I find myself *inquired of.* Inquired of, that is, by *men* rather than by scholars. There is a man in each scholar, a man who inquires and stands in need of answers. I am anxious to answer the scholar *qua* man but not the representative of a certain discipline, that insatiable, ever inquisitive phantom which like a vampire drains him whom it possesses of his humanity. I hate that phantom as I do all phantoms. On the other hand, the questions asked by human beings have become increasingly important to me. This is precisely what I meant by "cognition and knowledge as a service": a readiness to confront such questions, to answer them as best I can out of my limited knowledge and my even slighter ability.[34]

It is doubtful that, after 1945, Rosenzweig would have substantially changed this view with regard to the Jew as metahistorical. An open look at Rosenzweig's statements on and attitudes toward Zionism, particularly in connection with the theory in the *Star,* supports this conjecture. Rosenzweig was not a Zionist himself, and this, too, was an issue for which he was maligned. Yet, in a letter of 17 May 1927 to the reform rabbi Benno Jacob he wrote:

And you and I, at any rate, do not owe the fact of our existence and our being Jews to those self-satisfied citizens of the Diaspora but to the contemporary and later Tannaim of Palestine. Just exactly how I think the messianic future will be I find myself unable to formulate. But that is no proof against it. When the time comes, the details will fall into place. I am not naïve enough to imagine that peace among peoples and groups can come about without a radical change in human nature, a change which, contemplated from the present, must appear in the light of a miracle. That I have faith in that future I owe to the Siddur and Mahzor. I cannot exclude Zion from this faith. Just how great, how Jewish, how "modern" a Palestine will be grouped around it, I do not know. But when the time comes, that this Zion—not a heavenly but a messianic and hence earthly Zion—will be surrounded by, in all likelihood, what is "modern" in the sense of the time, will not disturb me. As little as the paraphernalia of the "history of civilization" which is grouped around my mental image of biblical antiquity disturbs me. But also as little as I begrudge the Palestine of today its factories and automobile roads. It belongs to it.

To what? To men, and these men are what I can see even today. And, if my impressions are reliable, among the Zionists there are better Jews than among us—theory here, theory there. You will probably agree to this.[35]

Rosenzweig speaks of his "beeline" theory, which the *Star* represents, and which he subsequently stood by:

Theory is invariably only a line. The roads of life deviate more or less, to right or left, from the beeline of theory. That line indicates only the general direction; anyone who insisted on walking the straight line could not move from the spot. Nevertheless, the beeline is still the right one; the road to the left and the road to the right (to which small-scale maps reduce the network of roads shown by General Staff maps) are in reality as little negotiable as the beeline, and are moreover theoretically false simply because there are two of them.

What I came to an understanding of in 1913, and wrote down in 1919, in the third volume of the *Star of Redemption* is the beeline. Everything I have done, including the very act of writing down and publishing, as well as all that followed: Academy, Lehrhaus, the founding of a home, the Jehuda Halevi book, the Bible, all this lies to the right of the beeline and can as little be construed in its details from the beeline as what the Zionist does to the left of it. To the right lies the Diaspora, to the left present-day Palestine. It would be a good thing if at least the leaders on both sides could see the beeline. Only a very few do, and rather fewer on the right than on the left. Nevertheless it works; the awareness is not so important as that.[36]

Thus, accompanying Rosenzweig's intention in "The New Thinking" to provide his first readers with the equipment of freshly cut keys for use in returning to the *Star,* lies the claim that his theory possesses its own integrity as an abiding philosophy that will hold true, that is to say, will be verified in actual life in spheres inclusive of the spiritual, the interpersonal, and the political.

"The New Thinkings'" Integrity

For all its inextricable bond to both the *Star* and the approximately six hundred readers in the 1920s, "The New Thinking" is a piece that can on certain levels be extricated from the book and audience and speak on its own. Besides and beyond its illuminations of some of the *Star*'s pages, it unlocks a treasure box of entrées into areas of interest directly related to, but not found in, the *Star* itself. Here Rosenzweig divulges some of its background. His brief mention of some of his influences, among them Feuerbach, Schelling, Buber, and Rosenstock-Huessy, leads one to a wealth of further discovery with regard to tracing the speech-thinking way of doing philosophy.

Rosenzweig's statement that his Notes to poems by Jehuda Halevi supply an example of the practical application of his *Star*'s theory opens the door to a world of ninety-two profoundly reflective philosophic-religious essays.[37] One finds also embedded in the Halevi book a small but glittering jewel set between the poems and the notes: an important essay on Rosenzweig's philosophy of translation.

"The New Thinking" stands on its own not merely because of its interesting content. In forbidding its publication in any future edition of the *Star*, Rosenzweig was holding to a speech-thinking principle. The essay pertained to a designated audience. A speech-thinker maintains that everything authentically spoken or written, to be authentic, must be intended *for* someone specific, so that that other may respond and render the initial speech full word. Thus, when it is to be read, this has to be done under separate cover: the *Star* and "The New Thinking" are separately spoken. The question nevertheless may be asked, once a piece of writing, a text, is out of the hands of the originator, is it still his or her "property"? Is it not a like a work of art whose viewing (outside of censorship) or reading is for anyone who wishes to do so? And in whatever context one wishes to view or read it? Is it not also fitting in the speech-thinking method that one can pick up another's speech and see it as directed specifically to her, in the specific context of what she was questioning or thinking about anyway? Did Jehuda Halevi write for (to) Rosenzweig? Rosenzweig, in his practical application, picked up Jehuda Halevi's hymns and poems and read them as if he were one of the designated audience. And, of course, he was. At any rate, the history of "The New Thinkings'" published editions has rendered it, even with respect for the author's wishes, a piece for anyone's eyes, for these editions have given to it, or imposed upon it an independent status. It appeared in German four times over a span of about sixty years. Written in February 1925, that is, four years after the publication of the *Star*, it was published for the first time that same year in the journal *Der Morgen*. The following year, 1926, it was included in *Zweistromland*, and in 1937, in *Kleinere Schriften*. Its next appearance was not until 1984, when the third book of the welcome monumental collection of Rosenzweig's writings became available: *III Zweistromland: Schriften zu Glauben und Denken*. In addition, breaking the silence between 1937 and 1982, an English translation of excerpts from "The New Thinking," which comprises about half of the essay, appeared in Nahum Glatzer's book of 1953 that introduced Rosenzweig, in panoramic fashion, to the English-speaking world.[38]

A foreword accompanied the 1925 publication, provided by *Der Morgen*'s editor, Julius Goldstein. He writes:

> The following contribution by Franz Rosenzweig belongs to the essentially new and spiritually decisive, the making known of which is one of the tasks of this Journal. Accordingly, the objections had to be silent which sadly reach my ear now and then with the words "too difficult." *The Star of Redemption*, with which this essay deals, is one of those rare works that are destined to give a jolt to the philosophical enterprise. Not

everyone loves and tolerates such a jolt. Those among the readers of this Journal, however—and there are quite a number of
them—who do not avoid the responsibility for the eternal
questions of mankind, will bring home ample profit—as long
as there is appropriate attentiveness to the subject—and will
view the *Star of Redemption* with fresh eyes. The difficulties in
understanding this work are based on the fact that the author
avoids all polemic that would allow us to recognize wherein
consist the new features and the ones divergent from all earlier features of his reflective work. And yet, to quote Goethe,
there is a polemic thread "in every philosophical writing, even
if it is hardly visible." This polemic thread the following essay
makes visible.[39]

"The New Thinking," of course, as a piece with its own
integrity, needs ultimately to be read of a piece. This is particularly so if a reader wants to ascertain whether he has problems and questions similar to those that had been raised by first
readers in order to avoid getting unnecessarily stuck in thorny
bramble patches that have already been cleared.

The Time-Releasing Effect of the Old Thinking on the New

One grave error in the understanding of a basic aspect of
Rosenzweig's way of doing philosophy has been repeated so
often that it seems to be sticking as a fixed idea about the philosophy itself. Rosenzweig has been criticized again and again
for remaining in part, and even in the main, a Hegelian logi-
cian and rationalist, that is, a German Idealist, in spite of
Rosenzweig's own statements to the contrary. He is said to be
a Hegelian unconsciously, or against his own conscious will.

Rosenzweig was awarded a Ph.D. in 1912 for his dissertation on Hegel and the state, and the claim persists that Hegelian thinking remains the actual method used in the *Star,* even though, in the *Star* itself Rosenzweig argues that traditional philosophical inquiry has been in ruin-heaps since 1800.[40] And within the first few pages of "The New Thinking," Rosenzweig specifies how he makes the move from the Old to the New Thinking.

Rosenzweig describes clearly and precisely how and why the new direction in his philosophic system makes its move away from the realm of traditional philosophy. Indeed, in part 1 of the *Star* Rosenzweig does, self-consciously and fully intentionally, use the method of traditional philosophy. But in his use of it he already makes apparent that the path will lead out of and away from, but, nota bene, *via* the old thinking. Because he takes the path *via* the old thinking, he takes along something out of it with him in his move to the new.

Part 1 of the *Star* deals with essences. It describes the essences of what Rosenzweig calls the three irreducible elements of reality: God, man, and world. Because the inquiry here is into essences, and not into what is happening, chronology is not a factor. Whether the task of trying to define God's essence is taken on before or after that of the world or of man is of no relevance. But because questions of timeless essence are the domain (and expertise) of traditional philosophy, the traditional method is applied here. Doing this, describing the essences of the three elements of reality, shows the purpose of traditional philosophy, its legacy, its value. It sets the scene for what is to happen in the story. The old thinking serves to introduce the characters and those specific features inherent in them that will not change throughout the story. But the old thinking, only in the light of the new thinking, is pre-story; it is pre-time. In the old thinking, the search for essences is not connected to time. That seemingly slippery variable is not wanted in formulations aiming to be timeless. Only *upon* the old thinking can the new begin, albeit far away. The old was necessary for the birth of the New. Thus, unlike "pure" old thinking, part 1 is self-consciously and deliberately—not time-less—but before and at the point of creation of time. Still, nothing has happened, and nothing can happen in part 1. Only: the elements are described, as to their inner workings, prior to actualized being, and they come to be, into being, into being-there, but not yet into relationship with one an-other. The story can open only in part 2.

Yet already here in part 1, for all its reliance on the old method, certain speech-thinking principles regarding time are plainly evident. First, we learn in time. Knowledge is nurtured by time. Knowing itself is not timeless, and therefore it does not stop at, and is in turn not restricted to, definitions of essences. Knowledge is more than knowing what "is." Ways of coming to know include more than the boundaries delineated by tra-ditional philosophy. Epistemological categories involve more than ontological categories and more than reason. Knowing takes time, partly because we do not know what is going to happen. Traditional philosophy set aside events and happen-ings, an individual's inevitable death, for instance, because not to do so would require a philosophy that takes account of real, lived time. Traditional philosophy wants to be timeless, to rel-egate Chronos to misty nonimportance, and to have timeless definitions, and to know essences, Being behind being. Rosenzweig writes in "The New Thinking": "Above all then: make haste! Do not stop! The important part is still to come! . . . What is written here is still nothing other than simultaneously leading the old philosophy *ad absurdum* and its salvation. Perhaps I will make the intention of the first volume clearest to the reader if I try to explain this apparent paradox" (*NT*, 73).

These views of the new use of the old are also clear in the *Star*'s pages, but perhaps to most readers are so only after the guidance given in "The New Thinking." Even though a crisis in the tradition had been recognized and vitally addressed by several philosophers struggling after Hegel—philosophers who were greatly admired by Rosenzweig and whom he calls the "point of view philosophers,"[41] notably Kierkegaard, Schopenhauer, and Nietzsche—the majority of intellectuals were still in Rosenzweig's time (and are still in many circles today) practicing, teaching, and living out of what had already been achieved, and thus for many decades have been a thing of a now dankly stagnating past: German Idealism.

Rosenzweig turns away from this old method whose further growth out of its depleted soil was now impossible. All attempts to foster growth resulted only in higher piles of debris that were creating unhealthy living air.[42]

Rosenzweig therefore surveys the ground for fresh territory, for breathing space for man, God, and world, philosophically and theologically. He finds land for ailing Philosophy in a region that will prove fertile only if equally ailing Theology agrees to be its neighbor. Side by side, with no confusion of the integrity of either of these two distinct disciplines, both theology and philosophy, according to Rosenzweig's method, would revive, and even flourish. Theology would derive vital strength from a dependence on philosophy's enquiry into the origin of things, namely, creation.[43] The once desiccated blood of philosophy would flow again, enriched by the transfusions from theology's notions of revelation. Philosophers of the method would thrive living in the vicinity of and in conversation with theologians, in a good neighborly fashion, always on speaking terms, but always also with a respected fence to protect the irreducibility of their respective properties.

Rosenzweig's formulation of his dynamic philosophic method arises from a believing philosopher's standpoint. He calls his new method variously the experiential method, the grammatical method, and, most emphatically, the speech-thinking method.

Thus, the New Thinking does not intend to denigrate the way in which philosophy had been traditionally pursued. Nor is it a breaking-up and overturning of the two-thousand-year-old Western tradition. To Rosenzweig, as to others, the tradition was already broken. He is not an iconoclast, but rather a builder. Rosenzweig's comments on part 1 have been repeatedly overlooked by some readers, either because the essay was not ever read, or not read in its entirety. Rosenzweig's comments here on part 1 explain the reference in Goldstein's foreword to the "polemical thread."

Rosenzweig's request that the essay never appear between the same covers as the *Star* has been stated as conforming to a principle of speech-thinking, that is, that there is always a specific speaker and a specific addressee(s). When cognizant of the fact that as new readers we are listening in on others' conversation, however, "The New Thinking" is interesting for all readers of the *Star.*

The New Thinking Beyond Franz Rosenzweig

Rosenzweig's desire to renew thinking and speech so that it would reincorporate, in human speech, the eternally fresh event and experience of God's word and response in time, was that desire and no more. He did not want credit for the "new thinking" but simply "new thinkers." Indeed, he wrote to his mother on 5 October 1921, when he heard that someone had cited him in a sermon and had called the *Star* "the sublime book of a new thinker who lives in our midst." He disclosed to his mother the following hope: "But it won't be really good until they use me in sermons without quoting me, and best of all, without even knowing that it is me they are using."[44] The fulfillment of this hope may still be a long way off. Rosenzweig himself was aware, already long before he saw the need to write "The New Thinking," that the *Star* would be only slowly received. To Gertrud Oppenheim, on 30 August 1921, he wrote: "One must also be able to write deliberately pedagogically; and that that writing is necessary has just recently become evident to me. . . . People believe of a person only just what is published, and the *Star* is difficult and will only come to be known gradually."[45] When Emmanuel Levinas, for example, states, in connection to his own work, "We were impressed by the opposition to the idea of totality in Franz Rosenzweig's *Stern der Erlösung,* a work too often present to be cited,"[46] he has not fulfilled that particular hope of Rosenzweig's for anonymity. Levinas is wholly conscious of his debt to Rosenzweig. This statement and reaction by Levinas must not be construed as what Rosenzweig ultimately intended with his introduction of "speech-thinking" into philosophy. What Rosenzweig wanted, with a sense of passionate urgency, was that the new thinking become a pervasive method for viewing the world and a way of living human life, without most people even knowing Rosenzweig's name, in the way that dualistic worldviews filtered down and spread through entire epochs, on a popular level, without most people even knowing Plato's name.

Levinas's statement of his indebtedness to Rosenzweig with regard to the opposition to the idea of totality reveals, *in nuce,* what Levinas writes about and attends to in virtually all his works. That reductive line of thought which annihilates otherness and which had been transported up through the centuries from Greek Iona to European Jena had resulted in the entangled ball of totality that exploded in World War I. A new line of philosophical thought, according to Rosenzweig, had been urgently needed from 1800 on, from the time of Hegel's successful drawing of the line to a circular close. Rosenzweig's "new thinking" offered a way out, a way to go on. The way, he writes in "The New Thinking," in his turn of indebtedness, pointed out to him by Eugen Rosenstock-Huessy, was conceived before World War I, bitterly confirmed by it, and became all the more pressing after 1918. The connections between the two World Wars, as well as today's wars in Europe, on the one hand, and totalizing, reductive philosophies, on the other, are undeniable. In the teens and twenties of this century Rosenzweig was of course not the only "new thinker," nor were new thinkers restricted to those in his circles and ken.[47] The longer the old thinking prevails beyond its time, the more pressing it becomes to pave practical avenues for the new.

Perhaps indeed the soil most fertile for the new thinking is North America. The individual who played the greatest role in planting the seeds in America from the vast areas of Rosenzweig's thought is, as noted, Nahum N. Glatzer (1903–1990). Paul Mendes-Flohr delivered the address at the dedication of the Nahum N. Glatzer Archives, Brandeis University, on 13 October 1992. He describes nuances of tensions in notions of newness, and inadvertently depicts how fitting it is that Glatzer was the one to introduce Rosenzweig. "Indeed, I believe Glatzer saw scholarship in general as a form of spiritual resistance to the moral distortions and conceits of our age: its imperious practicality, its cult of what Jacques Maritain called 'chronolatry,' the idolatry of what is newest or latest in time, our tendency to displace integrity with ambition and a quest for power and success."[48] Rosenzweig, who has seemed peculiar to European thinkers for using biblical texts as presuppositions for philosophizing, may seem less peculiar to North Americans, with their biblical sensibilities and mindset as dominant over the classical. In Professor Mendes-Flohr's tribute to the meticulous care with which Glatzer engaged in scholarship, reference is made to Rosenzweig's tying of scholarship to redemption:

Abstracted from the present, the details examined by the scholar, are, in a sense, rendered timeless. No one was perhaps more alert to the strange paradox of the timelessness of historical research—a paradox because of the historian's wont to place all in its proper temporal context—than Glatzer's mentor, Franz Rosenzweig. He explained the paradox as resting in the dual effect of scholarship to bind one to the past and *pari passu* to a proleptic vision of redemption:

> For "the turning of the hearts of the fathers to the children" is, according to the Prophet Malachi, a final preparation for the last days. Without scholarship each generation would run away from the preceding one, and history would seem to be a discontinuous series (as in fact it is) and not (as it ought to appear) the parable of a single point, a *nunc stans* (as history really is at the final [eschatological] moment, but thanks to scholarship . . . appears to be already in advance, here and now).

I am not sure whether Glatzer would subscribe to Rosenzweig's eschatological assessment of the scholar's vocation.[49]

The future cannot be told, though there can be faith in the final future, and this, to the faithful, can be told and actively worked toward. Philosophers who work with a faith in this final future gather up prescriptive principles in their philosophies. One who is chief among this type is Ludwig Feuerbach, whom Rosenzweig credits in "The New Thinking" with the discovery of speech-thinking.

Early Reviews of the *Star* and Rosenzweig's Responses

Among the reviews of the *Star* written between 1921 and 1925, two require special attention. These are the ones by Margarete Susman-Bendemann and Hans Ehrenberg. Of Susman-

Bendemann's review Rosenzweig wholly approved, of Ehren-berg's almost wholly.

Margarete Susman-Bendemann's review appeared under the title "Der Stern der Erlösung" in the 1921–1922 issue of *Der Jude*.[50] Upon reading it, Rosenzweig writes enthusiastically to her in February 1922:

> finally I have "Der Jude" and, in spite of the difficulties of writing in bed, I'd like to say a word of thanks.
>
> How profoundly you have understood the book, the follow-ing will prove it to you: the saying which you have placed as a motto above your essay,[51] I wrote in November '18 with the wholly clear awareness that it is the core and central sentence of the whole. I still recall the remarkable feeling with which I ran around that day. This must be how a mother feels when she feels her child moving for the first time. You have now expressed this secret of the book without profaning it. And your whole essay is like this. I thank you from my heart.[52]

Hans Ehrenberg's review was printed in the *Frankfurter Zeitung* on 29 December 1921. Rosenzweig responded at once:

> Your essay in the *Frankfurter Zeitung* is wonderful. I would have deleted only the next to last paragraph (not merely as author of the *Star,* but as critic of your critique).[53] It is stylistically so out of place that one would think you'd interpolated it after-wards. So leave it out if you put the essay into your collected works. It is, besides, also wrong. The "life" in the last word is *not* an opposition to "*philosophy.*" That is not at all any longer

the point. In this life there can also be philosophizing throughout; why not? (I do it.) What does *not* happen any longer is only the "looking" [*Schauen*]. The *view* [*Schau*], not the philosophy, is the opposition here out of which life springs. This is written with entirely clear words there, and I do not know how you could have overlooked them in reading, where you yourself have so strongly seen the challenge of the philosophy of life. The intention is anti-mystic, not anti-intellectual.[54]

Of all Rosenzweig scholarship, these two reviews, together with the author's own supplementary essay to his book, serve to draw us all to a more successful understanding, and perhaps even enactment than before, of worthy, if difficult, thinking.

PART ONE

Framing *The Star of Redemption*

2

"Germ Cell" of *The Star* *of Redemption*

FRANZ ROSENZWEIG

Letter to Rudolf Ehrenberg of 18 November 1917

D. R.,

I have in the meantime, it is now already a month ago, gained something important; at least it so appeared to me at first; now I've become doubtful again, because the usual mark of such discoveries, rabbitlike breeding of applications, has failed to appear this time, but there may be outside reasons for this. Namely: my long sought after philosophical Archimedean point. Perhaps you still remember: it was the first day of our

"'Urzelle' des Stern der Erlösung," in Franz Rosenzweig, *Der Mensch und sein Werk: Gesammelte Schriften,* vol. 3, *Zweistromland,* ed. Reinhold and Annemarie Mayer (The Hague: Martinus Nijhoff, 1984), 125–38. The footnotes are those of the editors.

Harz Mountain trip in 1914. We had just stepped out of a pinewood forest, and were talking about whether and how, in a purely philosophical way, or even only generally by some evident criteria, one could mark off from all characteristically human knowledge the boundaries of revelation. I knew nothing further than the sign of the "unwillingly," of the "*Ecce deus fortior me qui veniens dominabitur mihi,*" the fact that "the Prophet, a hunted quarry, fights against the image that gradually rises up before him." A presupposition then, that man by himself follows only "his drives," and that the voice of God continually summons him in just the opposite direction. Certainly not absolutely false, but much too paltry, and moreover really convincing . . . only for people who no longer have any real interest in the purely philosophical criteria. I did feel the insufficiency at that time, but all reflection about what was meant and intended as the central concept: the concept of revelation (it was not my fault that a programmatic acknowledgment of this concept remained at that time unpublished in the essay "Atheistic Theology," which, by the way, I read aloud to you in the Harz), so, all reflection always brought historical-philosophical results, never purely conceptual ones. Last year in the correspondence with Rosenstock I asked him outright what he understood by revelation. He answered: "Revelation is orientation." After revelation there is an Above and Below in nature—"Heaven" and "Earth"—which is real, and can no longer be relativized (here you see how what Rosenstock calls nature is, in spite of him, not the nature of natural science, but the nature of *poetry;* this is how everything that he demands regarding more natural-scientific method in the arts should be understood—but back to the issue): and a real firm Earlier and Later in time. Thus: in "natural" space and in natural time the center is always the point where I happen to *be* (ἄνθρωπος μέτρον ἁπάτων);[1] in the revealed Space-Time-World the center is an immovable fixed point that I do not displace whenever I myself change or move away: the Earth is the center of the world, and world history is before and after Christ (θεὸς καί λόγος αὐτοῦ μέτρον ἁπάτων).[2] This is roughly it, not literally, merely the outline; but a thought of stupendous simplicity and fruitfulness and certainly correct (I wouldn't trust myself if I didn't *also* arrive at it from my own position). Then why is it still not enough for me? For although I recognized it clearly, I was not yet satisfied for myself. Obviously because the unrest in my intellectual clockwork is called "1800" ("Hegel" and "Goethe," namely, the absolute self-consciousnesses of the two, of Hegel as the last philosopher, the last pagan brain, and of Goethe as the—you know the Eckermannlogion—first Christian as Christ had wanted him, that is to say, the first "human being pure and simple";—the "great pagan" and the "decidedly non-Christian" mean oddly enough nothing other than that Eckermannlogion, but they can only be understood by means of it). And thus I must look at everything if it is to become totally transparent to me, from what is, my intellectual center-point; on any other path my understanding quickly runs aground.

Now do not expect anything new. On the contrary. Perhaps nothing is new here except my feeling of now having a transparent coherence of thoughts, where before only *aperçus* thrust forth one before the other. Thus, only the "systematic" (in Weizsäcker's sense). And even that—well, I will see.

So, I say: philosophizing reason stands on its own feet, it is sufficient unto itself. All things are comprehended in it and in the end it comprehends itself (the only epistemological act against which nothing can be said, because it is the only one that does not occur according to the form A = B [which is the form of the cognition of reality and the form of reality], but according to the form of *logical* cognition A = A). After it has taken everything into itself and proclaimed its exclusive existence, the human being suddenly discovers that he, who has after all long been digested philosophically, is still there. And indeed, not as a man with his palm branch—that one the whale swallowed long ago, and, consequently, he can now while away the time singing Psalms in the belly of the whale—, but as "I who am after all dust and ashes." I, the quite ordinary private subject, I first and last name, I dust and ashes, I am still there. And I philosophize, that is: I have the gall to philosophize the sovereign ruler Philosophy. Philosophy has not yet directly told me (dust and ashes), but only through the man with his palm branch: I, first and last name, have to be altogether completely quiet, and then she shamed that man with his palm branch, through whom she has shamed me, shamed him and made him quite small in the face of a few ideals, and then she let the ideals sneak off into the absolute—and now suddenly I come as if nothing had happened to me, and light up the whole like Grabbe in the last act. *Individuum ineffabile triumphans.* The astonishing thing is not that the individual philosoph-izes, but that he is still there at all, that he still dares to yap, that he "izes."

Man has a twofold relationship to the absolute, one where the absolute has him, but still a second where he has *it*. Now what sort of a relationship is this second one?

I notice in rereading that this beginning is too full of hurrahs. So "again the same": Not merely is reason the ground of reality, but there is even a reality of reason *itself.* That reason substantiates reason *itself* (νόηις νοήσεως,[3] the principle of the Hegelian dialectic), that indeed explains how it can make the claim to substantiate reality (Hegelian dialectic is thus the necessary substructure of the Kantian critique); thinking must substantiate itself if it is to substantiate being; the self-substantiation of thought is thus necessary only for the sake of the thinkability of being; but against it remains the suspicion that *irrespective* of this relationship to being the self-substantiation of thinking is a mere logical game. Just as for the sake of the reality of creation one, to be sure, must assume a creator and a self-sufficient (almighty) one; but whoever believes he can renounce the reality of creation and thinks he can have life in its colored reflection,[4] for him the almightiness of the creator is also a mere problem; from this one can see that the "being" of God must still be separated from his concept (self-sufficiency). Thus also the reality of reason must still be separated from its concept (self-consciousness, νόηις νοήσεως, Fichte's A = A). There is "in" (or better: "of") reason something outside reason, something that cannot be grasped by the concept of truth (because truth is always "a correspondence of the idea to the object" or expressed less in the manner of a presupposition: a correspondence between separated things, where the "separated things" may be now different things—A = B, standpoint of consciousness, critique—or even the same things—A = A, standpoint of self-consciousness, dialectic). This something of reason beyond (*logically* spoken: "beyond") reason is a unity that is *not* a unity of two: not to be formulated as an equation, but rather a unity *apart* from twoness, the equal sign in the two equations, but in distinction from its application there, not as equal *sign* but as *reality,* not hypothetically ("*if* between A and B or A and A there is a *relationship,* then that of equality"), rather categorically ("*there is* equality 'before' all possible relationship"). *Ecce realitas.* Just as there "is" a God before all relationship, the one with the world as well as the one with himself, and only *this* being of God, the totally unhypothetical, is the seed-point of the reality of God, that which Schelling, of whom (and of Hans) you naturally must have unceasingly thought, calls the "dark ground," etc., an interiorization of God, which *precedes* not merely his self-exteriorization but even his self (just as, as far as I know, the Lurianic Kabbala teaches; I told you about it once).

So, what I'm aiming at is: that the absolute—and now I am intentionally taking this most abstract of all its characterizations—stands between two relativities, one before it and one after it. The earth rests on the great elephant and the great elephant on the great turtle and so on *ad infinitum,* that is what naïve metaphysics taught; the earth rests on the great serpent and the great serpent supports itself by biting its own tail, that is what Hegel teaches and to be sure with this does give an exhaustive explanation of the system of the earth-serpent. But he does not explain why this system does not now fall as a whole. I say: It does not fall and it does not hover, for there is no space "whereinto" it could fall, "wherein" it could hover. The serpent itself fills all possible space; it is *just as massive* as the earth that rests on it.

The objection is obvious that it is inadmissible to call the reality "before" and "after" by the same name. The reality, for instance, of God and the reality created by God are of course two entirely different kinds. It is certainly two different kinds, that's just what I want to speak about, but how would this being of two kinds be so meaningful if language were not nevertheless right and it *also* of one kind. The man of philosophy and the philosophizing man are after all both "human beings"; the palm branch must not obscure that fact.

I now claim that everything that happens between the absolute and the relative "before" it is revelation, everything that happens between the absolute and relative "after" it is nature, world, or whatever you want to call it. That is, of course, only supposed to be a first rough approximate formula, nothing more. That it is not more is shown already by the fact that of course the two relationships cannot be so antithetically opposed as appeared here; for while the absolute indeed stands in "relationship" to the relative after it, it is essential for the relative before it, that at first the absolute stands in *no* "relationship" to it as such for the time being, rather this relative stands as it is, bent, out of kilter, dust and ashes, but even so *on its own feet;* it is not a B that only through the "=" sign takes on existence, rather it has its "=" already in itself and at itself and does not ask after any A. It is B = B.

But the A asks after *It.* The "dark ground" would never *give birth to* the Godhead, but would rather eternally doze in its dull B = B; but God can *beget* Himself out of it and only out of it, out of this truly nondivine B = B that wants to be for itself. The mere "within" of God is still unfruitful; only the interior*ization,* only the descent of God into his own depth is "beginning." Just as the one who philosophizes without philosophy is dead, although philosophy can become alive only when it descends down to him, who is independent of it, when it lowers itself into him and thus begins the process of philosophizing that concludes with the recognition of the absoluteness of philosophy and the existence-of-the-human-only-in-relation-to-it. A becomes active against B = B until this, as B = A, recognizes its dependence on it.

Yet no memory of A's activity remains for B, neither for the philosopher B nor for the creation B. For the end of this process is that B is systematically digested, drawn in. The "memory" of that presystematic life can remain for him only when B is something that, even within the system, still rattles the system's cage-bars. One such B, however, is unique among all conceivable Bs: the free personality. The honest concession that freedom is the "miracle in the world of appearance," already by itself makes Kant personally the greatest of all philosophers; all others try to dodge it more or less; he alone expresses it, he alone has not forgotten through businesslike association with the truth how to be a child and a fool. Once freedom is accepted as that which cannot be captured in "relationships" and therefore cannot be systematized—*then* freedom may readily be defined as integration, submission, and so on—if only it remains in the "memory" that "*previously*" it was freedom pure and simple. And this living ἀνάμνησις[5] of the concept of freedom in Kant is for this reason the caravel on which alone we can discover the *nuovo mondo* of revelation, if we have embarked in the harbor of the old logical world. The "originary ground," the "being of God," the "reality of reason" (not in the Hegelian but in the Hansian sense), even the "one who philosophizes" (insofar as he is not simply "human")—all these we reach with our thinking only as limit concepts; we discover the "human" alone also in our thinking in its full translogical, dull, clumsy B = B-ness. Thought *touches* the other B = B concepts, this alone it *knows*. On it alone therefore can that prelogical process where the A "asks" after the B = B (see above) be demonstrated and only on analogy with that which is demonstrated here can similar processes also be opened up for the other B = Bs. Man pure and simple, the one who "is still there," with whom I began just a little while ago, is *really* the beginning.

This human being says: I. Only insofar and because the human being is not merely B but also B = B, can he say *I,* and among all Bs he is the *only one* that can say it; of all other Bs one can well claim *per analogiam* that they can say it, but precisely only *per analogiam;* directly they are not I's, but He–She–It, and even the human being himself, insofar as he is conceived as B, is merely a He–She–It. All relationships take place only between third persons; the system is the world in the form of the third person; and not merely the theoretical system, but just as man himself becomes an object, as soon as he wants *to make* something with or of himself, *he steps into the third person,* he stops being I (first and last name), he becomes "the human being" (with his palm branch). For the human being as B in this theoretical-practical system of third persons even God is only in the third person, only A. Although he *knows* of Him as a limit concept, that He essentially is A = A, only the A is valid however for its relationship to him (A = B). Spinoza writes of this human being—and Goethe subscribes to it—that he who loves God may not demand that God love him in return. After all, how could he?! In the purity of his bosom there surges an aspiration to give himself voluntarily to a Higher Purer Unknown One out of gratitude—it is a love in the third person, the He gives himself up to the It, no You becomes audible, and thus there one cannot speak of an I, and only the I can "demand" love; and in this world of the third person God is the sole It upon which, at least as a limit concept, the light of I-ness shines down ($A = A$), as those strange comparatives express it, "high*er*," "pur*er*": only a reflection, only an unknown is revered, the I that stands *behind* that It ($A = A$ beside the A of the usual equation $A = B$). All love here is surrender, a surrender whose simile can be *any* surrender of any kind; he also feels that he is partaking of "such a" blessed height when he stands before "it," and he who possesses "science and art," he "*also*" has religion. Because there is $A = A$, $A = B$ can be the dominant world-formula: all Bs related to each other, surrender everywhere, each can occupy for the other the place of the A (the left side of the equation), as well as "it" and "art and science" and even the human being himself can place himself on the left side of the equation and make himself the A for other things of the world; under the protection of $A = A$ *any* $A = B$ is possible and justified; and there is only one thing this eternally concrete B *cannot* do: demand that God love it in return. Because, for this, it would have to be able to make itself into an I, to identify itself with the $A = A$, not merely the A.

But the human being who does do this is the one who did not get into the objectifying thicket of relationships, the human outside of the theoretical-practical system, the human being as I. He may and must demand that God love him back. Indeed, he must demand that God even love him first. For his I is dull and dumb and awaits the redeeming word out of the mouth of God, "Adam, where are *you?*" in order to requite the first You that asks aloud for him with the first half-audible,

hesitant I of modesty. In I and You and again I this relationship is set in motion, as is the former relationship in the un-
determined He She It of general surrender. In the I of
revelation, and in the You of the question of conscience, or of
the command and response in Adam's I of modesty, or in Abraham's I of readiness, and backwards again in the I of repen-
tance and in the You of prayer and in the I of redemption.
Between the one B which is like no other B (the B that is not
B_1, B_2, B_3 and so on), rather is only itself and only like itself—B = B—and between A = A there is only one single-
tracked connection; there is no net, no system of relationships,
of real and of possible ones, where every junction can become
B and every one can become A, more accurately: where everything *can* become a junction and nothing *must* become one;
this is the world without a definite center point, the world of
Right and Left, of In Front and Behind, where everything can
become at any moment right and left, in front and behind and
a little wait-a-little changes the color of the future to the past;
the world whose sublime spirit teaches the human being to
know his brothers in the forest and shrub, and bush and water, and yet allows him—connected herein and herewith in an
unmediated way—also to feel that nothing perfect was given
to the human being. Instead of these brothers who are easily
and cheaply everywhere to be found, and to whom he stands
in "relationship," the human being has in the "connection" at
first only *himself* as an equal; the saying about neighborly love,
there a well-tempered matter of course, here becomes a voice
of trumpets, for it is not said to the human being in the purity
of whose heart surges an aspiration for voluntary *surrender* but
to the deaf I, buried in its own I-ness, to this I, about which

nothing can be presupposed except this: that it loves *itself.* But that is why, *after* this word has first opened up the deaf ear, the human being now recognizes in the neighbor the one who also is really like him, recognizes him not merely as B_2, B_3 and so on, as one who dwells beside him in the same world, fellow-member of the great equation $A = B$, of which after all he knows only that which he *sees*—for he recognizes him only as It, only as his brother in forest and grove, in rock and water; rather I recognize that he *is not He She It, but rather an I,* an I as I am, not one who dwells beside me in the same directionless and centerless space, not a travel acquaintance on the journey through time without beginning and end, but my brother, the consort of my destiny, the one for whom "things are" exactly as for me, who also sees only the one track before him as I do; my brother not in the world, in woods and grove, bush and water, but in the Lord. All Bs are made brothers, for all are interchangeable with each other, every B can become the A to the other. Not even once does the thought-bridge lead from $B = B$ to other $B = B$s: the bridge, the $=$ sign, is constructed in the $B = B$ itself, it does not lead out of it. Only that from One $A = A$ the Word went out to $B = B$, only this leads $B = B$ out beyond itself, and only in this *event* that happened to it can it think another $B = B$, to which the same thing has happened, a neighbor, who is like You. Not out of his own essence [*Wesen*] and out of the purity of his own heart does he discover the other, but out of the *happening* which happened to him and the deafness of his heart.

"Essence" is the concept under which the world of objects, the world of $A = B$, arranges itself—essence, the universal, which gathers all singulars under it, because it "precedes" all that is singular. Because it knows that human beings in general, "all" human beings, or the world in general, all things, are brothers to each other, *for this reason* the Stoic "loves," the Spinozist "loves" his neighbor. Against such love that arises out of the essence, the universal, stands the other that rises out of the event, that is out of the most particular (thing) there is. This particular goes step by step from one particular to the next particular, from one neighbor to the next neighbor, and denies love to the furthest until it can be love of neighbor. The concept of order of this world is thus not the universal, neither the *arche* nor the *telos,* neither the natural nor the historical unity, but rather the singular, the event, *not beginning or end, but center of the world.* From the beginning as well as from the end the world is "infinite," from the beginning, infinite in space toward the end, infinite in time. Only from the center does there arise a bounded home in the unbounded world, a patch of ground between four tent pegs, that can be posted further and further out. Only seen from this viewpoint do beginning and end change from a concept of the boundedness of the infinite to cornerstones of our world-possession: the "beginning" becomes the creation, the "end" the redemption.

Revelation is then capable of being a *center* point, a fixed, immovable centerpoint. And why? Because it happens to the *point,* to the motionless, deaf, immovable point, the defiant I, the "I am when all is said and done." My "freedom," and to be sure not my freedom as the philosophers lie about it, in that they draw off from it the red blood of arbitrariness and let it run into the vessel of "sensuousness," of "drive," of "motives," and admit as freedom only the bloodless residue of obedience to the law. Rather the total freedom, my full, dull, irresponsible arbitrariness, my whole "this is how I am when all is said and done," without which every freedom of philosophers is lame from birth. For of what use is all obedience to the ideal, all acceptance of universally valid maxims, all Hegelian godliness, if the human being, of whom all these beautiful things are expected, is without strength? But more: if he is not so strong such that in this his sinful naturalness he does not know himself master of all these ideals that demand his service, and in all his pointlike quality [*Punkthaftigkeit*] first finds the courage to put the period [*Schlusspunkt*] at the end of every sentence of the system of morality. But how does he attain such strength and such courage?

The "ideals," "imperatives," "ideas" *et hoc genus omne* speak to human beings: Surrender to me! out of "gratitude," "voluntarily," so that you "become who you are," fulfil your "destiny"—but in any case: surrender to me! A presupposition then, that the human being gives up that which is proper to him. Against this, revelation says: Do my will! work my work! Presupposition then, that which is proper to God, the will of God, the work of God is entrusted to the human being so that he might do it. What a paradox this, seen from the standpoint of the world! That which is the Highest, instead of demanding our surrender, surrenders itself to us; instead of raising us to its height, it lowers itself to us; and again, instead of promising us ourselves as reward ("become who you are"), it promises us the undoing of self, nearness to God as blessedness. The human being therefore, to whom God entrusts himself, to whom he, who is elevated and humble in one, lowers himself—the human being receives, by making room for God in himself, all that surrenders to God, even himself, the human being. All surrender in the world flows to God as the idea of ideas, and God, in that for his part he gives himself in revelation to the human, brings to him as dowry all worldly submission. Thus, the human being becomes powerful through the revelation of his own submission to the ideals. The ideals are many. One blocks the light to the other. The law of the exchangeability of all objects in the A = B world is valid also for them; the human, placed between them, knows with certainty only that he should surrender himself, but not to which of them. The tragedy of the conflict of duties reigns. God's command is an order, calling out clearly to this human being and in this situation of this human being; countering with a question or lateral switches to another track of the system are impossible; for here there is no system of lines, only the one two-track route; at most Lucifer's defiance or Jonah's flight would be possible. There is clearly a *kingdom* of ideals (which is only systematiz-*able,* thus not *capable* of unity); but only one *Word* of God (which *develops* into the manifoldness of the kingdom). For this reason in the world of revelation no "conflict" is valid. The legend begins where the tragedy *ends*—with the fifth act.

Thus, no "law" is given to the pious one, for he stands under an "order." An order that gives him full powers over the whole world and its ideals. But certainly an order. His arbitrariness has to be silent. Not fundamentally: the "giant battle of duty," the discord between "ideal and life" and so on does not belong here; such fundamental differences are rather the characteristic of the systematizable world, of the world of A = B, no matter whether we develop this world one-dimensionally in *opposites* with Hegel, or multidimensionally in *relationships* according to the tendency of our time. No battle of this kind that can somehow be understood as a general concept is ordered for the pious person. Rather, as the order itself remains as an order bound wholly to the person and to the moment, so now also its realization in the world enters not into a universal opposition, but into the specific one: not, for instance, does "the" duty oppose "the" love, rather *this* duty and *this* love thrusts aside every other duty or every other love. Revelation thrusts itself as a wedge into the world; the This battles against the This. Hence, the prophet's resistance to his mission, his struggle against the gradually rising image, is not to be confused with moral struggles. The higher in this case does not fight the lower, but *that which is commanded fights all else that would merely be possible,* in spite of the fact that even the "High" belongs to this possible, any comparison, any ranking into the system of higher and lower does not exist. The mission releases the prophet from the "ideal" as well as from "life" and drives him into the *conceptless* world, into a world in which A = B has lost its validity and everything appears to him as B = B. His "nature," which rebels against the divine charge, is by no means "nature" in some opposition to something better; rather it is his whole human being, the "better one" and the "worse one" in an undifferentiated mixture; it is his wholeness, his secret will toward a *system* that fights against the intrusion of the commanding word; the "system" in him, the secret "life of Goethe," struggles for its self-preservation, B = A against B = B.

The foregoing shows that there are relationships between revelation and world, not merely in thinking—that would already result from the "formulas"—but also in reality. And thus the relationship of B = B to A = B is an aggressive one, aimed at transformation. The relationship of A = B to B = B, however, is only a theoretical-skeptical (unbelieving) one, which is content with a mere new interpretation, with an explanation of B = B as "actually" A = B. Thus, it is also content at every moment, while B = B can be content only at the "end"; only at the end is the "unity" of the "system" replaced by the "community" of "all," all power and order (A = B) by selfhood and immediacy (B = B); this is why at the "end" also for revelation the problem of the "brothers in woods and grove, in rock and water," which is solved easily and cheaply with emotion at every moment by pantheism, becomes real, and its solution, which is necessary precisely for the sake of the really accomplished all-ness, is promised *per miraculum*. Unbelief has for its legal basis the consciousness that B = A is only the "spiritualization," the "truth" of B = B; it thinks it possesses B = B in its concept of ὕλη,[6] which is an error; for every concept of ὕλη *is* already a "spiritualization" as opposed to the presence B = B, which is totally without concept, totally without unity, *is* thus already A = B; all the same, it *is permitted* to commit this error; as regards the main point, it is correct in that its B = A really somehow "means" B = B (the human being with his palm branch is *somehow* one with the I, i.e., first and last name). And just this "somehow one," which was expressed from the start by the sameness of the letters in the formulas, also produces the possibility for the faith that moves mountains or more simply: the possibility of the pious persons *living* his faith. If the world were not A = B, but instead A = C, then such a possibility could not be conceived. Only because the pious person and life are both of one blood, only because it is merely asked of faith to transform the world (so to speak, back) into *its own* chaos, only for this reason is the work of revelation on the world possible. At the moment, however, where B = B is at an end with this work, where thus *all* B = A has become B = B, then B = B, in that it has become "all," has lost its most particular essence, to be an unopened something buried in itself. There is no longer being in the face of God: God is One and All.

Thus, the following picture emerges: the different relationships that I discussed rhapsodically side by side at the start, explaining one through the other, without being able clearly to demarcate them from one another, now are mutually arranged. They are—both the "human being, who is still there" (in spite of the "one with his palm branch of ideals"), the "one who philosophizes" (in spite of "philosophy"), and the "originary ground" (in spite of the "personality of God")—all are concepts of *pure factuality.* I would be able to symbolize them as relationships by the proportion-stroke /. Thus

$$A = A \mathbin{/} A = A$$
$$A = A$$

$$B = B \mathbin{\underline{\hspace{2em}}} A = B$$

$$A = A/ \longleftarrow \qquad\qquad A = A/$$
$$B = B \qquad\qquad\qquad B = B$$

Don't be alarmed! The symmetry is not as great as you think at first glance. Above all:

$$A = A/$$
$$B = B$$

I should actually have written only in parentheses separately; for it quite coincides with the

$$A = A$$
$$/$$
$$B = B$$

of the triangle; for revelation is already itself the relationship of "pure factuality." Altogether different on the right side of the triangle. It designates the result of the idealistic movement: the I = I as the key to the I = Not-I, *Hegel's* concept of the "spirit," Goethe's "Is not the core of the world to be found in the human heart." This recognition still had to be grasped itself as a fact, as a world-historical point: Hans's discovery of the "philosopher" and my concept of "1800," which after all also revolves around the philosopher in contrast to philosophy. The idea of immanence—and what else is paganism!—which Hegel theoretically and Goethe practically brought to perfection, has now itself become a *fact* and thereby can be grasped by revelation. This "pure factuality" is thus something for itself; it does not coincide with the side of the triangle, rather it is a philosophical *salto mortale* down from the philosophical cornerstone of the triangle—*mortale;* "1800" signifies an absolute end, or else, an absolute beginning; when Hegel discovered in himself the last philosopher, Goethe discovered in himself the first Christian; there is nothing to add.

That which takes place between the two base points of the

triangle, between simply human and simply world or between belief and unbelief or between theology and philosophy—the practical movement from left to right, the theoretical from right to left—that has already been stated; that the movement from left to right is the stronger one and is sure of final victory, is reflected in the diagram in this: that on the right the *salto mortale* of factuality is an addition, a unique fact in the course of history, whereas the left side has the factuality in the blood and operates with its strength at every moment.

The *salto mortale* at the peak of the triangle is finally characterized as "the last one" in that above and below the proportion-stroke there stands the same thing. The pure factuality here is thus without movement, eternally. The eternal happening in God can be discerned, as is shown by the figure as well as by the history of thought, from two bases: from the basis of the perfected philosophy (Schelling) and from the basis of revelation (mysticism). In this way, *theo*logy and philos-*ophy* are joined, completing the triangle of the sciences—I myself am still astounded and reluctant about this thought—by theosophy.

The rest is philo-logy, that is, silence. But seriously, what do you think of it? It has become more complete and richer than I myself expected. But in contrast to that time in the Harz Mountains, I am *myself* convinced. And I think you are, too; it is after all formulated only for you; even if I wanted to formulate it for Rosenstock, I would have to write it entirely differently and by the way would not after all have enough distance from it at the moment to write it differently. I wrote it εἴς σε βλέπων,[7] and possibly, as you are a "November man" and I mean: of the second half, it will reach you on your birthday. In any case you must keep it to yourself, for in this form it cannot yet bear any other eyes.

Now, after the happy clucking yesterday right after laying the egg, I read the whole thing through again today. It requires a great quantity of good will to understand it. For the terminology on the first pages is still entirely labile; I would be able to improve it now from the end, but that would mean writing anew, and, among other things, it is too cold for me here. You must try to glide along with the labile quality. B = B means exclusively the human being only from a certain point on; during the comparatively very complicated mustering of the forces, it still means, also translogical reality, the transpersonal Godhead. But I think you would have to notice this in the reading, just as I after all noticed it only in the writing. I am virtually certain even today of the fruitfulness of the whole thing, in spite of the many mistakes and present lack of clarity. But now I'm starting to cluck again, and that was pardonable only yesterday.

One more thing: concerning influences, I must bring in still another besides those named: Christoph Schrempf (do you know him?) with his early, probably first work on Kant and Christ, wherein he corrects the opposition of autonomy and heteronomy through that of law and command.

I am very surprised at the exceptional position of mysticism *between* real theology and real philosophy. Perhaps that is the unstrained solution for many historical difficulties—Plotinus,

India, et al. I had never actually wanted to take an interest in the Steiner theosophy up to now (accordingly I know only what was written about it in the two Meyrink novels and awhile ago in the *Christlichen Welt* (Christian world), but perhaps I will do so now. But now really the end.

Your F.

3

"The New Thinking"
A Few Supplementary Remarks to the *Star*

FRANZ ROSENZWEIG

Formerly, I let *The Star of Redemption* be published without a foreword. The vestiges of the usual forewords by philosophers frightened me off with their cackling after the egg had been laid and their discourteous invectives against the reader who after all had not done anything so far,—who could not even have read the book yet. Even the tranquil Kant did not escape this danger, not to speak of his noisy followers right down to Schopenhauer. The following pages are not at all meant to make up for the mistake I happily avoided at that time, nor are they ever again to be printed in future editions of the book

"Das Neue Denken," in Franz Rosenzweig, *Der Mensch und sein Werk: Gesammelte Schriften,* vol. 3, *Zweistromland,* ed. Reinhold and Annemarie Mayer (The Hague: Martinus Nijhoff Publishers, 1984), 139–61.

whether at its beginning or at its end. They are the response to the reverberation that the book has aroused in the four years that have elapsed since its appearance. Not to its rejection; that would not be like me. But precisely to the acceptance which it has found. Where one has not found an open door, one has lost nothing; but where one is welcomed kindly and with honors, there one may—indeed to be decent one must—after having enjoyed hospitality for a time under a conventional introduction and, accordingly, in the forms of conventional courtesy, at the opportune hour unmask one's own face, and thus call forth the critical moment when out of the conventional relationship the personal relation emerges—or does not. With full awareness that, with this act of truth that one day may become necessary, one of course risks the agreeable atmosphere of the social relationship that one had simply enjoyed up to then.

If I disregard the small circle of those who could have written the book just as well or better than I, then the book really owes the acceptance that it has found till now altogether to such a "social misapprehension": it has been bought and—worse—read as a "Jewish book." It passes unread and, worse yet, when read, is taken to be the book about the part of Jewish youth that in various ways endeavors to find its way back to the old law. As far as I'm concerned, that's perfectly alright. What the Pharisees of the Talmud and the Holy Men of the Church have known: namely, that the understanding of man reaches only as far as his deeds, clearly applies to the honor of mankind to being understood as well. But, as far as the book is concerned, out of that prejudice arise several—unnecessary—difficulties for the readers, and for the buyers a—very necessary—disillusionment. The following pages are an attempt to ease somewhat those difficulties for the readers and, likewise, to assuage somewhat the disillusionment of the buyers who believed they were purchasing a nice Jewish book and afterwards, like one of the earliest critics, had to discover that it is not at all "made for the daily use of every member of every family." I cannot describe *The Star of Redemption* more correctly than that critic has done with concise brevity: it is really not intended for the everyday use of every member of the family. It is not a "Jewish book" at all, at least not what those buyers who were so angry with me take for a Jewish book. It does deal with Judaism, but not any more exhaustively than with Christianity and barely more exhaustively than Islam. Neither does it make the claim to be a philosophy of religion—how could it do that when the word "religion" does not occur in it at all! Rather, it is merely a system of philosophy.

But, to be sure, the system of a philosophy that as such grants to the reader, to the expert just as to the layman, the fullest right of disapproval. Namely, a system of a philosophy that does not just want to bring about a mere "Copernican turn" of thinking, after which he who has carried it out sees all things turned around—yet still only the same things that he has seen before. But, rather, thinking's complete renewal. I would not say this if I had to say it only about my book and not about the thinking, which I do not credit myself with having discovered nor even at present to be the only one teaching. On the contrary, common sense has always thought this way, and among contemporary thinkers more in any case than would be dreamt of today by Ueberweg-Heintze. What has just been said is by no means a recommendation of the book, more likely the opposite. For neither the expert nor the layman wants something new. The former is happy if he can continue as he has learned—otherwise he would not be an expert. And the latter, should he become "interested in philosophy," likewise does not want to be presented with a new and revolutionary one, but with the "right" one, the "philosophy of the present"—otherwise he would not be a layman. And, since the reading public is composed of these two groups, I am permitted to have said what I said without the fear of having recommended my own book.

According to hallowed custom, a system of philosophy consists of a logic, an ethic, an aesthetic, and a philosophy of religion. *The Star of Redemption,* in spite of its three volumes, breaks with this custom—it was only because of publication difficulties at the time that it was combined into one volume, and in accordance with the publisher's promise, beginning with the second edition it will once again revert to the original division into three volumes. Indeed, it contains, apart from the fourth of these ingredients proper to a system's punch, all the others: the logic, particularly in the second book of the first volume, in the first book of the second volume, and in the third book of the third volume; the ethic, in the third book of the first volume, in the second and third books of the second volume, and in the first book of the third volume; the aesthetic, in all books of the first and second volumes and in the second book of the third volume. But as this curious distribution reveals, the systematic principle of this philosophy is a different one. The title itself attempts to point to this principle by combining in one astronomical image the headings of the three volumes—Elements, Path [*Bahn*], Form [*Gestalt*]. And it is precisely this transition from the usual to the new way of putting the question which the formulations of the first volume that became so quickly infamous accomplished, to which I now turn.

The reader has a particularly high regard for the first pages of philosophical books. He believes they are the basis for all that follows. Consequently he also thinks that in order to have refuted the whole, it's enough to refute these pages. Hence the immense interest in Kant's teaching of space and time, in the form in which he developed it at the beginning of the *Critique*. Hence the comical attempts to "refute" Hegel by refuting the first triad of his Logic, and Spinoza by refuting his definitions. And hence the helplessness of the general reader in the face of philosophical books. He thinks they must be "especially logical," and understands by this the dependence of every succeeding sentence on every preceding one; so that when the famous one stone is pulled out, as a consequence "the whole collapses." In truth, this is nowhere less the case than in philosophical books. Here a sentence does not follow from the preceding one, but more likely from the one following. Whoever has not understood a sentence or a paragraph is little helped if, in the conscientious belief that he must not leave anything behind that is not understood, he reads it perchance again and again or even starts over again. Philosophical books deny themselves such a methodical ancien régime–strategy, which thinks it may not leave behind any fortification without having conquered it. They want to be conquered napoleonically, in a bold attack on the enemy's central force, upon the conquest of which the small outlying fortifications will fall automatically. Thus, whoever does not understand something can most assuredly expect enlightenment if he courageously goes on reading. The reason why this rule is difficult for the beginner, and, as the cases cited above show, also for many a nonbeginner to accept, lies in the fact that thinking and writing are not the same. In thinking, one stroke really strikes a thousand connections. In writing, these thousand must be artfully and cleanly arranged on the string of thousands of lines. As Schopenhauer said, his entire book wants to impart only a single thought which, however, he could not impart more briefly than in the entire book. Thus, if a philosophical book is worth reading at all, it is certainly so only when one either does not understand its beginning or at the very least misunderstands it. For otherwise the thought that it imparts is scarcely worth re-considering [*Nachdenken*], since one evidently already has it, if one knows right at the beginning of its exposition "where it is leading up to." All this is valid only for books; only they can be written and read without any consideration for the passing of time. Speaking and hearing follow other laws. Of course, only real speaking and hearing, not the kind that derogates itself a "lecture" and during which the hearer must forget that he has a mouth and becomes at best a writing hand. But, at any rate, for books it is so.

Just where that decisive battle of understanding is fought, where the whole can be seen at a glance, cannot be said in advance; in all probability already before the last page, but hardly before the middle of the book; and surely not by two readers at precisely the same point. At least when they are readers who read on their own and not readers who, because of their learning, already know before the first word what is written in a book, and because of their ignorance do not know it even after the last one. In respect to older books, the last-mentioned readers' virtues are most often found in two sorts of people, professors and students; in respect to newer ones they tend to be found in one and the same person.

With that we are back again at *The Star of Redemption*. Everything just said concerning the reasonable way of reading the beginnings of philosophical books applies especially to its first volume. Above all: rush! Do not stop! The important part is still to come! And the difficult part, for example, the concept of the Nothing [*Nichts*], "the Nought" [*der Nichtse*], which here appears to be only a methodological heuristic concept, reveals its inner significance only in the short concluding passage of the volume and its ultimate sense not until the concluding book of the whole. What is written here is still nothing other than the reduction *ad absurdum* of the old philosophy and, simultaneously, its salvation. Perhaps I can best clarify for the reader the intention of the first volume by trying to explain this apparent paradox.

All philosophy has asked about "essence" [*Wesen*]. This is the question by means of which it differentiates itself from the unphilosophical thinking of common sense, which does not ask what a thing "actually" is. It is satisfied with knowing that a chair is a chair; and it does not ask whether it might, actually, be something quite different. But this is what philosophy asks when it asks about essence. The world, by no means, may be world; God by no means God; man by no means man; but all these must "actually" be something quite different. If they were nothing else but really only what they are, then philosophy—God forbid!—would ultimately be superfluous. At least, a philosophy that wants to attain something "completely different."

That is after all what all earlier philosophy wanted, as far as my university knowledge of it extends; and if I can trust my exacting and dutiful quarterly examination of the *Kant-Studien,* the ravens are still flying around the mountain (and regrettably still find young finches who, notwithstanding their own beautiful beaks, try hard and, unfortunately successfully, to caw like them). Tirelessly, still, the possibilities of the "reduction" of some given one, to its given other are still playing through all permutations, which can broadly be characterized by the three epochs of European philosophy— cosmological antiquity, the theological Middle Ages, and our anthropological modern era. Especially, of course, the pet idea of the modern era: the reduction to "the" I. This reduction or the "grounding" of the experiences of the world and God in the I that has these experiences is still today so self-evident to scientific thinking that anyone who does not believe this dogma but prefers to reduce his experience of the world to— the world, and his experiences of God to—God, is simply not taken seriously. This philosophy considers reduction overall as something so self-evident that if it troubles itself to burn a heretic, it prosecutes him only because [he is guilty] of a forbidden kind of reduction, burning him at the stake as a "crass materialist" who says: everything is world; or an "ecstatic mystic" who says: everything is God. That someone might not at all want to say "everything 'is' . . . " never occurs to it. But in this What is? question, applied to "everything," lies the entire error of the answers. An is-sentence must, if it is worth the bother of saying it, say something new after the "is," something that was not there before. So, if one asks such is-questions in regard to God and the world, one must not be surprised when the "I" emerges—after all, what else is left! Everything else, the world and God, has already been disposed of before the "is." And likewise, when the pantheist and his *Associé,* the mystic, discover that the world and man are of divine "essence," or when the other firm, of the materialist and the atheist, finds that man is only a product, and God nothing but a reflection of "Nature."

In truth, these three first and last subjects of all philosophizing are onions, which one can peel as much as one likes—one finds always only onion layers, and not anything "entirely different." Only thinking necessarily gets off on the wrong foot as a result of the altering power [*verändernde Kraft*] of the little word "is." Experience, no matter how deeply it may probe, will discover again and again in man only what is human, in the world only what is worldly, in God only what is divine. And only in God that which is divine, only in the world that which is worldly, only in man that which is human. Finis philosophiae? If it were [the end], so much the worse for philosophy! But I do not think that things will be as bad as that. On the contrary, it is at this point, where philosophy to be sure would come to the end of [its way of] thinking, that experiential philosophy [*erfahrende Philosophie*] can begin.

In any event, this is the point of my first volume. It wants to teach nothing more than that none of these three great basic concepts of philosophical thinking can be reduced to one of the others. In order to make this teaching emphatic, it is given in a positive form: it will not be shown that none can be reduced to the other two, but instead the reverse, that each can only be reduced back to itself. Each is itself "essence" [*Wesen*], each is itself substance—with the entire metaphysical weight of this expression. When Spinoza, at the beginning of his work, passes on the scholastics' concept of substance to the great idealists of 1800—on this point he is the great mediator between two epochs of European thought, precisely because he did not understand it theologically as the past epoch had done, nor anthropologically as the coming one would do, but rather cosmologico-naturalistically, and by this he formalized it and thus made it transformable—, he defines substance, as everyone knows (here this impudent phrase may for once be written without making the reader blush, for he usually knows, as we have seen, the first sentences of philosophical books) as that which is in itself and is comprehended through itself. There is perhaps no better way for me to explain the intention of the difficult constructive parts of the three books of the first volume than to say that here, for each of the three possible bearers of the concept of "essence," it is shown how it in its special way fulfills this definition. What I refer to as "yes" corresponds to the "*in se esse*" of Spinoza's definition; what I refer to as "no" to the "*per se percipi*." Naturally it is not implied that they are the same. In this whole essay I am giving the reader of the book only pointers. If he wants to know what is in it, then he must read it. I cannot spare him that.

But in any case I believe that with what I have just stated, I have characterized the tendency of the first volume, as well as one can do that as an author—that is, certainly less well than an intelligent reader can do. As to the question of the essence of things there can only be tautological answers. God is only what is divine; man only human; the world only world. However deeply one digs into them, one will still find again and again only these things themselves. And this holds equally for all three. The concept of God does not by any means have any special status. As a *concept* of God it is no more unattainable than the concepts of man and of the world. The reverse: the essence of man and the essence of the world—the essence!—is no more within reach than the essence!—of God. About all of them we know equally much or equally little. That is to say, everything and nothing. We know in the most exact way, know with the intuitive knowledge of experience what God, what man, what the world "is," each taken separately; and if we did not know that, how could we talk about it, and, above all, how could we "reduce" the two given ones to the given other, or deny the two other given possibilities of reduction. And we certainly do not know in the underhanded way that thinking knows—the way in which it "turns things into something other than they are" [*"verandernden" Wissen*], in what sense God, in what sense the world, in what sense man are different than they are. If we did know that, how could that intuitive knowledge maintain itself to the extent that it does against such knowledge, so that again and again it coaxes us from this question, these attempts at reduction? Specters disappear when the cock of knowledge crows; these specters never disappear. That we believe that the one of these essences is closer to us, the others farther away, is based, in much the same way as is the related misuse of the nonsensical words immanent and transcendent, on a confusion of the essences with the realities God, world, man. Between these nearnesses and distances, approaches and withdrawals indeed obtain; but they do not ossify into essential characteristics [*seinshaften*] so that God, for instance "would be" transcendent. No, rather as essences, God, world, man, are all equally transcendent with respect to each other, and in regard to them as realities one cannot say what they "are" except only—but that does not belong here yet.

But now then, what do we know of them apart from and between that "everything" and "nothing"? At any rate, at least, something. Namely, precisely this: what we mean by the words divine, human, worldly. You see, with these expressions we mean something quite definite, such that one cannot be confused with the other. What do we mean then? Where do we find the three essences, which at the same time are unreal and plainly evident, in the way that these three adjectives set them off in their isolation from each other? Here a second motif becomes visible which interlaces with the first, the logical-metaphysical one, and which in this interweaving together with it dominates the structure of the first volume.

Where are such forms [*Gestalten*] that have essence yet lack truth, life, or reality? A God who is not the true one, and not real, a world that is not living and not true, human beings who are not real and not alive? Forms that do not know and do not want anything of each other, and of the two others? Shadows that do not dwell in the same space as our reality, our truth, our life, and which yet haunt everything that happens in our space? The reader can give the answer himself if he consults his knowledge of Spengler. Spengler's Apollonian culture grasps precisely those gods, worlds, human beings that are meant here. Spengler's concept of the Euclidean designates precisely the separation in essence, the "transcendence" with respect to each other, that is designated here. Only that Spengler, as usual, wrongly interprets what he has rightly seen. The mythical Olympus, the plastic cosmos, the tragic hero are not done away with because they have been; they have not "been" at all in the strict sense of the word; the real Greek, when he prayed, was, to be sure, not heard by Zeus or Apollo, but of course by God; and likewise undoubtedly he did not live in the cosmos, but in the created world, whose sun, our sun, also shone for Homer; and he was not a hero of Attic tragedy, but a poor human being like us. But in spite of the fact that these three forms never really existed, they are yet the premise of all our reality. God is as living as the gods of the myth, the created world is as much the real one, and so little mere "appearance," as the plastically closed finalities in which the Greek thought he was living, or in which as a political creature he wished to live, and which he as an artist had created around himself. The man to whom God speaks is just as much the true man, and just as far from being a repository of ideals as is the hero of tragedy in his stubborn defiance. The spiritual forms that, in world history, only here, only in Spengler's "Apollonian culture," were isolated and consequently became visible by this, are also contained in all their life as its secret, invisible premises, regardless of whether this life is older or younger, regardless of whether it has itself become historical form or has remained historically invisible life. That is the classicality of classical antiquity—and the reason why the first volume of the *Star*, by trying to set out the elementary contents of experience purified of the admixtures with which thinking would like to occupy itself must become at this very point a philosophy of paganism. This first volume itself now builds it up again out of historical forms according to the constructive derivation of the three "substances" [*Substanzen*], whereby the darlings of the moderns, the "spiritual religions of the Far East," come off badly.

Thus paganism is definitely no mere religio-philosophical bogeyman for adults, which is the way it is used by the orthodoxy of earlier centuries and, curiously enough, in Max Brod's recent well-known book. Rather it is—no more and no less than the truth. The truth, to be sure, in an elemental, invisible, nonrevealed form. So that wherever it tries to be not elemental but the whole, not invisible but form, not secret but revelation, it becomes a lie. But as an element and a secret within the whole and the visible and the revealed, it is everlasting. It endures as much as the great objects, the "substances" of thinking, in real, nonobjective and unsubstantial experience.

For experience knows nothing of objects; it remembers, it experiences, it hopes and fears. At most one could understand the content of the memory as an object; that would then be an understanding, after all, and not the content itself. For that is certainly not remembered as my object; it is nothing but a prejudice of the last three centuries that in all knowledge the "I" must necessarily accompany it; so that I would not be able to see any tree without the "I" seeing it. In truth my I is only present when it—is present; when, for instance, I must stress that I see the tree because someone else does not see it; then certainly the tree in my knowledge is bound up with me; but in all other cases I only know of the tree and of nothing else; and the standard philosophical claim that the I is omnipresent in all knowledge distorts the content of this knowledge.

So experience does not experience things, which, however, become visible as final factualities in thinking about the experience; but what it experiences, it experiences in these factualities. And that is why it is so important for a pure and full [re]presentation of experience to have displayed those factualities clearly and to have confronted thought's tendency to their confusion. They are the cast, the theater program, which is also not a part of the drama itself and which one nevertheless does well to read beforehand. Or in other words: the Once-upon-a-time with which all fairy tales begin, but precisely only begin, and which in the course of the fairy tale, in the flow of its narration, cannot occur again. The latter is actually the more accurate simile. For if the first volume answered the old question of philosophy: what is? and did it in such a way that the thus-far-and-no-further of experience has been called out to the drive for unity of philosophical thought, now experienced reality itself can be presented in the second volume. Not by the means of the old philosophy, which after all does not reach beyond the question about "that-which-is" [*"Seienden"*] (which is most often answered wrongly, but at best correctly)—and that which is real "is" not. Thus, the method of the second volume will have to be a different one, notably that of our last comparison: a method of narration. Schelling predicted narrative philosophy in the foreword of his brilliant fragment "The Ages of the World." The second volume [of the *Star*] attempts to supply it.

What does it mean to tell a story? He who narrates does not want to say how it "actually" was, but how it really took place. Even when the great German historian in his well-known definition of his scientific intention uses the former and not the latter word, he means it in this way. The narrator never wants to show that it actually was entirely different—it is precisely a sign of the poor historian, who is obsessed with concepts or craves sensationalism, to have that as his goal—rather he wants to show how such and such that is on everyone's lips as concept and name, for example, the Thirty Years' War, or the Reformation, actually happened. For him also something merely essential, a name, a concept, unravels, but not into something other that is equally essential, but rather into its own reality, more precisely its own realization. Is-sentences he will scarcely construct at all, and was-sentences, as we said, at best at the beginning; nouns, that is, substantives, do enter into his story. The interest, however, is not in them, but in the verb [*Verbum*], the time-word [*Zeit-wort*].[1]

Time, that is to say, becomes entirely real to him. What happens does not happen in it; but rather time itself happens. The sequence of the three books of the first volume was entirely accidental. Each of the four other possibilities would have been just as possible. Essence wants to know nothing of time. Now, in the middle volume, sequence is not merely important; rather, it is the truly important thing to be conveyed. It already is the new thinking of which I spoke at the beginning. When, for instance, the old [thinking] poses the problem of whether God is transcendent or immanent, the new [thinking] tries to say how and when He turns from the distant to the near God and again from the near to the distant one. Or when the old philosophy sets up the alternative determinism-nondeterminism, the new follows as it were the path of the deed [leading] from the conditioning of character and the tugging tangled growth of motives through the shining grace-filled moment of grace of choice to a must that is beyond all freedom, and thus overcomes the variations of that alternative, according to which man is constrained "to be" either a dressed-up piece of the world or a masked God. The new philosophy does nothing other than turn the "method" of common sense into the method of scientific thinking. Wherein then is the common sense different from the sick, which, exactly like the old philosophy, the philosophy of "philosophical astonishment" (astonishment means standing still) sinks its teeth into a thing and will not let go until it "has" it in its entirety? It can wait, go on living; it has no idée fixe; it knows: all in good time. This secret is the whole wisdom of the new philosophy. It teaches, in the words of Goethe, "understanding at the right time," as Goethe wrote:

> Why is truth far and distant,
> hiding itself in deepest depths?
> No one understands at the right time!
> If one did understand at the right time,
> Then truth would be near and spread out,
> And would be lovely and mild.

The new thinking knows, just like the age-old [thinking] of common sense, that it cannot know independently of time—which was the highest claim to glory that philosophy up to now assumed for itself. As little as one could just as well begin a conversation with the end, or a war with a peace treaty (which of course the pacifists would like), or life with death, one must learn rather for better or for worse, actively or passively, to keep waiting until the moment comes, and not skip any moment. So, likewise, cognition in each moment is bound to that very moment and cannot make its past not past, or its future not in the future. This is true of everyday matters, and everyone grants that. Everyone knows that for the attending physician, for instance, the treatment is present, the getting sick past, and the certification of death future, and that it would make no sense if out of the fancy of timeless knowledge he wanted to eliminate learning and experience in the diagnosis, cleverness and stubbornness in his therapy, and fear and hope in his prognosis. In the same way, no one who makes a purchase seriously believes that he can see the merchandise in the delirium of its purchase in the same way as afterwards, in the throes of regret. Yet this is equally true of the last and highest things that one generally believes can be discerned only timelessly. What God has done, what He does, what He will do, what has happened to the world, what will happen to it, what happens to man, what he will do—all this cannot be severed from its temporality, so that one could, for instance, discern the coming kingdom of God as one can discern the created creation or could be permitted to look upon creation as one is permitted to look upon the kingdom of the future; just as little as man may let the lightning bolt of what is always only present experience turn into the coal of the past, so little may he expect [*erwarten*] of the future, for it is always only in the present [*gegenwartig*], and to wait [*warten*] for it is the surest means of preventing it from striking; and just as the human deed is a deed only so long as it is still impending, and when done, only an event, indistinguishable from all others.

Thus the tenses [*Zeiten*] of reality are not interchangeable.[2] Just as every single event has it present, its past, and its future, without which it is not discerned, or only distortedly, so it is with reality as a whole. It too has its past and future, and, to be sure, an everlasting past and an eternal future. To discern God, the world, man, is to discern what they do or what happens to them in these tenses of reality. What they do to each other and how they are affected by each other. The separateness of their "Being" is presupposed here, for if they were not separate, they could do nothing to each other; if "in the deepest depth" the other were the same as myself, "deep down," as Schopenhauer would have it, I could not love him, but only myself; if God were "in me," or "only my higher self," the dogma of an assistant barber that must, along with the other [dogma], that He is the whole in all its glory, needs to be underwritten at the initiation into many a youth organization, that would be no more than a useless verbal obfuscation of an otherwise clear relationship; but above all, this God would hardly have anything to tell me since I know already what my higher self has to tell me. And if a man were "godly," as one inspired German professor proclaimed under the influence of Rabindranath Tagore's mantle, then the path to God that stands open to every human man would be blocked to this man. This is how important the presupposed separateness of "Being" is, of which, however, no more will now be said. For in the only reality we experience, it will be bridged and all that we experience are experiences of such bridge building. God himself, if we want to comprehend him, conceals himself; man, our very self, shuts himself in; the world becomes an apparent puzzle. Only in their relationships, only in creation, revelation, redemption, do they open up.

And now this great world-poem is retold in three tenses.

Actually told only in the first, the book of the past. In the present the story yields to the direct exchange of speech, for of those who are present, be they human beings or God, they cannot speak in the third person, they can only be heard and addressed. And in the book of the future there reigns the language of the chorus, for even the individual grasps the future only where and when he can say We.

Thus the new thinking's temporality gives rise to its new method. In all three books to be sure, but most visibly in the book that is the heart of this volume and thus of the whole, in the second, the book of the present revelation. The method of speech takes the place of the method of thinking, as developed in all earlier philosophies. Thinking is timeless and wants to be timeless. With one stroke it wants to make a thousand connections; the last, the goal, is for it the first. Speech is bound to time, nourished by time, [and] it neither can nor wants to abandon this ground of nourishment; it does not know beforehand where it will emerge; it lets itself be given its cues from others; it actually lives by another's life, whether that other is the one who listens to a story, or is the respondent in a dialogue, or the participant in a chorus; thinking, by contrast, is always solitary, even if it should happen in common, among several "symphilosophers": even then, the other is only raising the objections I should actually have made myself,— which accounts for the tediousness of most philosophic dialogues, even the overwhelming majority of Plato's. In actual conversation something really happens. I do not know beforehand what the other will say to me, because I do not even know beforehand what I will say; perhaps not even whether I will say anything at all; it could well be that the other begins, that being most often the case in the genuine conversation; a fact of which one will easily be convinced by taking a comparative look at the Gospels and the Socratic dialogues. Socrates most often just sets the conversation in motion, on the course of a philosophical discussion. The thinker plainly knows his thoughts in advance; that he "expresses" [*ausspricht*] them is only a concession to the defectiveness, as he calls it, of our means of communication; this does not consist in the fact that we need speech, but rather in the fact that we need time. To need time means: not to be able to presuppose anything, to have to wait for everything, to be dependent on the other for what is ours. All this is entirely unthinkable to the thinking thinker, while it alone suits [*entspricht*] the speech-thinker. Speech-thinker—for of course the new, speaking-thinking is also thinking, just as the old, the thinking thinking did not come about without inner speaking; the difference between the old and new, logical and grammatical thinking, does not lie in sound and silence, but in the need of an other and, what is the same thing, in the taking of time seriously. Here, "thinking" is taken to mean thinking for no one and speaking to no one (for which, you can substitute "everyone," the so-called "general public," if you think it sounds better). But speaking means to speak to someone and to think for someone; and this Someone is always a very definite Someone, and doesn't merely have ears like the general public, but also a mouth.

In this method, there is concentrated whatever renewal of thinking can come of the book. It was first discovered by Feuerbach, then introduced again into philosophy through the posthumous work of Hermann Cohen, although he was certainly unaware of its revolutionary power. Those passages in

Cohen were already known to me when I was writing; but it was not to them that I owe the decisive influence for the book coming about. Rather, it is to Eugen Rosenstock to whom I am indebted, whose now published *Angewandte Seelenkunde* [Practical knowledge of the soul] had lain before me in a rough draft copy for a year and a half when I began to write. Since then, aside from the *Star*, yet an additional fundamental presentation of the new science has appeared in the first volume of Hans Ehrenberg's published work on Idealism, his *Fichte*, also written in the form of genuine discussion proceeding through time; Viktor von Weizsäcker's *Philosophie des Artzes* [Philosophy of the doctor] will appear in the foreseeable future; Rudolf Ehrenberg's *Theoretische Biologie* [Theoretical biology] subsumes the doctrine of organic nature for the first time under the law of the real, irreversible time. Independently of those mentioned and of each other, Martin Buber in *Ich und Du* [*I and Thou*] and Ferdinand Ebner in *Das Wort und die geistigen Realitäten* [The word and the spiritual realities], a text produced at precisely the same time as my work, made their own advance on the focal point of the new thought, the one that is treated in the middle book of the *Star*. Instructive examples of the practical application of the new thinking are contained in the notes to my *Jehuda Halevi*. A precise and profound knowledge concerning all these things is enclosed in the foundation stones of the powerful, mostly unpublished, works of Florens Christian Rang.

Theological interests, among all those just mentioned, have helped in the breakthrough of the new thinking. All the same, it is not theological thinking. At least not at all what one up to now had to understand as such. Neither in aim nor in means. Neither is it directed only at the so-called "religious problems" which it handles instead in the course of, or rather along with logical, ethical, aesthetic ones. Nor is it familiar with that attitude characteristic of theological thinking in which attack and defense are mixed together, and never calmly turned to the matter. If this is theology, then, in any case, it is just as new as a theology as it is [new] as a philosophy. The introduction to the second volume deals with this question, as overall the three introductions try to show the reader the ways that lead out of his familiar spiritual world into the world of the book. Theology may not debase philosophy to the [role of] handmaiden; but just as degrading is the role of the cleaning woman which philosophy in modern times and the recent past had accustomed itself to attribute to theology. The true relationship of the two renewed sciences, as the above-mentioned introduction develops it, is that of siblings, indeed it has to lead to the point where both are united in one person. The theological problems are to be translated into the human, and the human driven forward until they reach the theological. The problem of the name of God, for example, is only part of the logical problem of names in general, and an aesthetics that gives no thought to whether artists can find salvation is indeed a well-mannered science, but also an incomplete one.

Completeness is after all the true verification of the new thinking. From the perspective of the old [thinking], its problems are for the most part simply invisible and, when they impinge on its vision, are not recognized as scientific problems. This is true not only of theological problems in the narrower sense but also of the majority of human ones that the grammatical method makes tangible for scientific comprehension,

as in the case of the logic of the I and You or for the just mentioned logic of the name. From the position of the new thinking, by contrast, the entire domain of the old [thinking] remains
observable and treatable. For instance, the problems of the old,
Aristotelian and Kantian logic persist as problems for speech-
thinking, but as problems in the form of the It. As such they
are treated in the first book of the volume, to be sure only in
a first orientation, but nevertheless removed already from the
false relationship to the I, and placed at least in outline into
the correct relationship: to a He, to Him.

God plainly did not create religion, but rather the world.
And when he reveals himself, the world not only continues to
exist everywhere, indeed it is hereafter for the first time really
created. Revelation does not in the least destroy genuine paganism, the paganism of creation. Not at all. It only allows the
miracle of return and renewal to happen to it. It is always present and, if past, then out of that past that stands at the beginning of human history,—revelation to Adam. Revelation as
"ever renewed" is the content of the second volume just as
paganism as ever enduring is the content of the first. It deals
with the visible and audible, thus manifest reality; its prede-
cessor deals with its dark-mute hidden presupposition. Of the
historical forms of revelation in their distinctiveness, that is, of
Judaism and its antipodal offspring, Christianity, there is as yet
no mention. Only because and insofar as both renew the "revelation to Adam," only to that extent is the new thinking Jewish or Christian thinking. And on the other hand, because and
insofar as paganism in its historical forms forgot or denied this
revelation to Adam, who was as little a pagan as a Jew or Christian, this historical [paganism], petrified in a specific form, is

of course not enduring; precisely in its separateness and having become form it no longer partakes of reality. The temples of the gods have rightly fallen, their statues rightly stand in the museum, their worship, as far as it was set in order and codified, may have been a single enormous error—but the invocation that called out to them from a tormented breast, and the tears shed by the Carthaginian father, who offered up his son as a sacrifice to Moloch, cannot have remained unheard, or unseen. Or is God supposed to have waited for Sinai or even for Golgotha? No, as little as there are roads leading from Sinai or from Golgotha by which he may be reached with certainty, so little could he have refused to meet even the one who sought him on the mountain trails surrounding Olympus. There is no temple built which would be so near to him that would permit man to be confident of this nearness, and none which would be so far from him that his arm could not easily reach even to there, no direction out of which he could not come, none out of which he had to come, no block of wood in which perhaps he does not at some time take up a dwelling, and no Psalm of David which always reaches his ear.

The extraordinary position of Judaism and Christianity lies precisely in that they, even when they have become religions, find in themselves the impulse to free themselves from this religiosity of theirs and to find their way back again to the open field of reality from out of their specialization [*Specialität*] and their fortification. All historical religion is from the beginning specialized, "founded"; only Judaism and Christianity had never initially been specialized and never in the long run something that had to become and be founded. They were originally something wholly "unreligious," the one a fact, the other an event. All around them they saw religion, religions. They themselves would have been most highly astonished also to be addressed as one. Only their parody, Islam, is religion from the very start and does not at all want to be otherwise; it is consciously "founded." The six places in this volume where it is dealt with thus represent the sole part in the book that is in the strict sense philosophy of religion.

But the "Jewish book"? as the very title seems to indicate? I would like to be able to speak as softly as the poet, when he concludes his powerfully far-reaching fugue on the theme of the cosmic beauty with the unforgettable preface: It appeared to me in the form of youth, in the form of woman,—to be able to say wholly truthfully what I now have to say. I received the new thinking in these old words, thus I have rendered it and passed it on, in them. I know that to a Christian, instead of mine, the words of the New Testament would have come to his lips; to a pagan, I think, although not words of his holy books—for their ascent leads away from the original language of mankind, not toward it like the earthly path of revelation— but perhaps entirely his own words. But, to me, these words. And yet this is a Jewish book: not one which deals with "Jewish matters," for then the books of the Protestant Old Testament scholars would be Jewish books, but one for the old Jewish words come in order to say what it has to say, and precisely for the new things it has to say. Jewish matters are, as matters generally are, always already past; but Jewish words, even if old, take part in the eternal youth of the word, and the world is opened to them, then they will renew the world.

But so the miracle remains that there is yet something that has form, and something that does not pass away. To be sure, not in the real world of the ever renewed life, where only the present is present, and the past only past, and the future only coming. But of these three, time in the most temporal sense is only the present. And as the forms of paganism project into the present, like a bygone creation, so too is the coming redemption anticipated in eternal forms. The flow of events projects gleaming pictures onto heaven, above the temporal world, and they remain. They are not archetypes. On the contrary, they would not exist did not the stream of reality continue to break forth out of its three invisible-mysterious sources. Those invisible mysteries themselves become image-like in these images, and the steady course of life devolves into recurring form.

Judaism and Christianity are these two eternal clock-dials under the week- and year-hands of time constantly renewed. In them, in their year, there is shaped in the form of a replica the course [*Ablauf*] of world time, which cannot be replicated, only experienced and narrated; in their God, their world, their human being, the secret of God, of the world, of the human being, which in the course [*Bahn*] of life can only be experienced, not expressed, becomes expressible; what God, what the world, what the human being "is" we do not know, but only what they do or what is done to them; but how the Jewish or the Christian God, the Jewish or the Christian world, the Jewish or the Christian human being look, that we can know exactly. Forms take the place of the existing substances [*seienden Substanzen*] which are perpetual only as secret premises of the always renewed reality, forms moving about that eternally mirror this always renewed reality. The third volume deals with these [forms].

The representation of Judaism and Christianity, contained

therein, is thus not originally determined by an interest in religious studies, but rather, as can be inferred from what has just been said, by a generally systematic one, especially by the question of an existing eternity, hence by the task of overcoming the danger of understanding the new thinking, perhaps in the sense, or rather the nonsense, of irrational tendencies such as the "philosophy of life," among others, everyone clever enough to have steered clear of the jaws of the idealistic Charybdis seems nowadays to be drawn into the dark whirlpool of this Scylla. Consequently the representation proceeds in both instances not from their consciousness of themselves, in the case of Judaism not from the law, in the case of Christianity not from faith, but rather from the external, visible form through which they wrest their eternity from time, in Judaism from the fact of the people, in Christianity from the event that founded the community. Only out of these do the law and faith here become visible. Thus, on a sociological basis Judaism and Christianity are placed side by side and up against each other. The result is a representation that does not do full justice to either, but, which having paid this price, goes beyond the usual apologetics and polemics in this area—indeed, for the first time. I have said elsewhere (in the essay "Apologetic Thinking") what there is to be said in this regard, and I need not repeat myself here.

The sociological basis on which the portrayal of Judaism and Christianity is based has further consequences in the sociological passages that are intertwined with their presentation. That the Jewish people is based on the fact that it itself is, and the Christian community on the event around which it assembles, leads in the former to a general sociology and in the latter to a sociology of the arts. Messianic politics, that is a theory of war, thus closes the first book of the volume, and Christian aesthetics, that is a theory of suffering, closes the second book.

And so, the treatment of the ethical and aesthetic problems comes to an end in the first two books through the forms of Judaism and Christianity. Both pervade all three volumes, but only here in the third are they satisfactorily separated into two books in the customary manner. That being generally the character of the volume, which in a very real sense steers [thought] back again to the channels of the old thinking with its questions about being. But the aesthetic of this volume shows that a peace has not yet quite been reached. Whereas the first volume treated only the traditional aesthetic principles, and the second volume, admittedly in its entire arrangement as well as in the final critical point, freed aesthetics from the connection—in this instance particularly strong because it remains unconscious—to the idealistic tradition, but nevertheless developed in the midst of that treatment, the usual content of an aesthetic, the third volume allows the principles to culminate in an applied aesthetic, and, in this vindication of art through applied art burns all ships that could carry one back again from this new land into the classical land of origin of the science of [taking] delight [in something] free of [any attendant] purpose.

I let myself linger relatively briefly on these things which essentially fill the first two books of the third volume; as these passages are supposed to be understandable to such a degree that one critic has recommended to the reader that he begin with the introduction to this volume and from there read backwards and forwards—to which advice I have no objection, provided that, from the "forwards and backwards" he finally leads also from the beginning to the end. And to the misunderstanding that is probably inherent in the reputed understandability, I believe I have in the preceding supplied some antidotes. All the same, there remains in all that is understandable and misunderstandable something that is genuinely not understandable. It is the same thing that must unsettle the simple [frame of] mind in the juxtaposition of Judaism and Christianity, and which as well startles the thinker who sees himself here called upon in utter seriousness, not in that provisional manner that still makes it bearable for him in the first volume, "to multiply that which is." It is the truth, then, that is at stake in the concluding book of the volume and of the whole, the Truth of which there can only be One.

One still thinks today that all philosophizing must begin with epistemologically theoretical considerations. The truth is that it will at best end with them. The archproponent of epistemologically theoretical prejudice in our day, Kant, with his *Critique,* is himself nothing other than such an ending, namely, of the historical epoch that began with the natural science of the Baroque. Only of the philosophy of this epoch does his *Critique* prove to be immediately true. Corresponding to the Copernican turn of Copernicus, which made man a speck of dust in the whole, is the "Copernican turn" of Kant, which, by way of compensation, placed him upon the throne of the world, much more precisely than Kant thought. To that monstrous degradation of man, costing him his humanity, this correction without measure was, likewise, at the cost of his humanity. Thus all critique comes only after the performance. As little as the theatre critic has anything to say beforehand, no matter how clever he may be, for his critique should not give evidence of the cleverness that he already possessed prior to the performance, but rather only of that which through the performance arose in him: just as little does a theory of knowledge which precedes knowing, actual knowing, make sense. For all knowing, if something is really known, is a singular act and has its own method. Methodological reflections about history in general replace one based on the singular historical work, as little as a literary historian's view of a drama replaces a newspaper reviewer's criticism that flows from the immediate impression of a performance,—or more appropriately still less, for in drama and performance at least the book is the same, but there is happily no "history in general." What is now true for every single work of science, namely, that it must go at its material with its own never previously applied methods and instruments if it wants to extract the secret of precisely this material, and that only the pupil allows his methods to be prescribed by the teacher instead of by the material, this is just as true for philosophy; only that, since, as a result of the comic circumstance that philosophy is a university discipline with chairs that have to be occupied, and freshmen that have *stud. philos.* printed on their calling cards; here pupils who never get beyond the schoolboy stage are so much the rule that they do not notice it until retirement at seventy and consequently consider the kind of theory of knowledge that, granted, is sufficient in their school exercises, as the only one.

A knowledge, out of which something comes, is exactly like a cake into which something has been put. Put into the *Star of Redemption,* for starters, was the experience of the factuality prior to all facts of real experience. Of the factuality that forces upon the thinking, instead of its favorite word "Actually," the primary word of all experience to which its tongue is unaccustomed, the little word And. God and the world and man. This And was the *alpha* [*das Erste*] of experience; thus it must also return in the *omega* [*im Letzten*] of the truth. Still in the truth itself, in the final truth, which can be only one, there must be an And; this truth, different [*anders*] from the truth of the philosophers, which is permitted to know only itself, must be truth for someone. Should it be then, nevertheless, the one truth, it can be truth only for the One. And thereby it becomes necessary that our truth is manifold and that "the" truth changes into our truth. Truth in this way ceases to be what "is" true, and becomes that which, as true—wants to be verified [*bewährt*]. The concept of the verification of the truth becomes the basic concept of this new theory of knowledge, which replace the old theories of noncontradiction and of objects and introduces in place of the static concept of objectivity of those theories, a dynamic one; the hopelessly static truths, as those of mathematics, which were taken to be the starting point of the old theories of knowledge, without then really going beyond this starting point, are here to be grasped as the—lower—limit, as rest is the limit of motion, while the higher and highest truths can be grasped only from this perspective as truths, instead of having to be labeled fictions, postulates, necessities. From those least important truths, of the type "two times two is four," on which people easily agree, without using up more than a little brain grease—for the multiplication table something less, for the theory of relativity a little more—the path leads over the truths that have cost man something, on toward those that he cannot verify except with the sacrifice of his life, and finally to those whose truth can be verified only by the commitment of the lives of all generations.

This messianic theory of knowledge, which evaluates truths according to the price for its verification and to the bond that they establish among human beings, cannot, however, lead beyond the two eternally irreconcilable expectations of the Messiah: the one to come and the one to come again,—it cannot lead beyond the And of these two final commitments on behalf of the truth. Only with God himself does the verification reside, only before him is the truth One. Earthly truth thus remains split—split into two, like the extradivine factuality, like the primal facts of world and man. These return together with their And into these ultimate facts that are Judaism and Christianity: as the world of Law and the faith of man, Law of the world and man of faith.

But now, in this return of the eternally invisible presuppositions of this experience in the final clarity of the supraexperienced truth, the true order of the three establishes itself. And by God becoming the head, the God of Truth, the last book clears up the confusion of the first, whose God not merely had no relationship to the world and man, but had not even a firm place, so that he could not signify the God of Truth, but only the false gods. Only the false gods had been able to appear there as the fulfillment of the concept of God, of the question: what is God? Now, since every concept of God has long since become as dark as the hidden God, and God himself reveals himself as Creator, Revealer, Redeemer, the First and the Last and the heartfelt [*der Herzmittengegenwärtige*] burn into one in the God of Truth. And of this God in whom real past Having Been and real present Being and real future Becoming crystallize together, we may—now for the first time—say: He is.

Here the book ends. For what is still coming is already beyond the book: "Gate," out of it, into the No-longer-book. No-longer-book is the enraptured-terrified recognition that in this beholding of the "world-image in God's countenance," in this apprehension of all being in the immediacy of a moment [*Augenblick*] and blink of the eye [*Augen-blick*] the limit of humanity is entered. No-longer-book is also the becoming aware that this step of the book into the limit can only be atoned for through—ending the book. An ending that is at the same time a beginning and a middle: to enter into the middle of everyday life. The problem of the philosopher goes through the whole book, especially through the three introductions. Only here does it find its definitive solution. Philosophizing should proceed further, indeed proceed further. Everyone should philosophize some time. Everyone should some time look round about from his own standpoint and his point in life. But this look is not an end in itself. The book is not a goal that has been reached, not even a preliminary one. It itself must be answered for [*Verantwortung*], instead of it carrying itself or being carried by others of its kind. This responsibility [*Verantwortung*] happens in everyday [*Alltag*] life. Only in order to recognize and to live the day as every-day [*All-tag*], the day of the life of the All [*All*] had to be traversed.

In the writing of these pages I have experienced that it is difficult as an author to speak about one's own book. The author may hardly presume to say something authentic. For he himself stands no differently than anyone else with regard to that which is spirit in his work and hence transplantable into other spirits. The other, because he is an other, and precisely because he is an other, will be permitted to attempt time and again—in Kant's bold assertion that really is not quite so bold—"to understand Plato better than he understood himself." I would not want to deny this hope to any of my readers. What the author himself has to say, even if he makes an honest effort to say it in the form of a commentary, is all too easily transformed into supplementary notes. These, in any case, in what they underline and bracket in the book, will depend on what has reached the author's ear as an echo. And they are thus also addressed only to the reader of today. And they will not satisfy even him, precisely in his contemporaneity. For that which he demands, and is after all permitted to demand, was precisely not given to him: the formulaic designation [*schlagworthafte Bezeichnung*] under which he could bury what he has possibly learned about the new thinking in the cemetery of his general education. It was not out of ill will on my part that I did not give him this slogan [*Schlagwort*], but simply because I don't know one. True, the work in which I sought to elucidate the new thinking objects to several slogans with a special antagonism that goes beyond the general tendency against all Isms; but should I therefore let the book be pinned down to the conventional counterparts of those Isms? can I do it? The designation that I would most readily have to settle on would be absolute empiricism; at least it would cover the special attitude of the new thinking in all three areas, of the primeval world of concept, the world of reality, the transcendent world of the truth; that attitude which likewise does not claim to know anything of the heavenly other than what it has experienced—but [to know] this really, even if philosophy already may besmirch it as knowledge "beyond" all "possible" experience; nor anything of the earthly which it has not experienced—but this not in the least, even if philosophy may already extol it as knowledge "in advance of" all possible experience. Such confidence in experience would be the teachable and transmittable aspect in the new thinking, if, as I certainly feared, precisely this confidence itself is already an indication of a renewed thinking—and if that just stated slogan is not itself one of the remarks, which, precisely because they come from the author himself, seem to the reader in some parts not merely simple, as surely many other comments do on the previous pages, but all too simple, and again in some parts more difficult than the book itself. Both are unavoidable. The greatest poet of the Jews already knew the former case when he lets the wise man reply to the heathen king: "My words are too difficult for you, therefore they seem too easy to you." And the greatest poet of the Germans knew the latter case, whose Mephisto, to Faust's impatient call, "there many a riddle must be solved," replies: "But many a riddle is also made."

PART TWO

The Star of Redemption in Review

4

The Exodus from Philosophy

MARGARETE SUSMAN

Und will das Licht sich dem Trübsten entwinden,
So wird es glühend Rot entzünden.

And if the Light wants to wrest itself from the deepest gloom,
It will inflame glowing red.

—Goethe

A peculiar life is commencing today in our country. At the moment when all the stars above it seem extinguished, and when its reality stares at us greyer and more wasted than ever, an odd lightning and flashing is beginning above it in the sky of its spirit, as if from new, unknown stars. Strange cloud formations and configurations of light gather above its head: Forms of pure inwardness arose, appearances foreign to every-

From *Frankfurter Zeitung*, on 17 June 1921, and in 1. *Morgenblatt*, no. 441.

thing that pertains to the life of the day, and yet finally determined and winged, again to descend to it. One asks oneself, in view of these manifold and yet essentially profoundly interrelated formations, whether it will not nevertheless at all times be Germany's fate [*Verhängnis*] and destiny [*Bestimmung*] to be thrown back again and again into its inwardness, whether its ultimate destiny cannot, despite all threats and dangers of annihilation—indeed because of them, be determined only in its inwardness. But it will certainly have to be a different inwardness than the one that until now left a place beside it to an outside that is entirely foreign to its essence, devoid of essence. Not an abstract one, ignorant of the world, like that born out of German Idealism, which shunned the wretched details of daily life, limited in their content, did not desire to penetrate its own life circle in order to live toward a goal that was beyond content and lay in the infinite—it will have to be an inwardness that, in equal measure, as conscious of itself as it is of the outside, that grasps the inside only as impulse and measuring rod, the outside as its task. And already there appears to have dawned in the colorfully glowing forms, which begin to wrench loose out of our deeply darkened atmosphere, the hour of a tremendous return.

What they all have in common is rebelling against any kind of philosophy in the sense of pure thinking: the conviction that no logic, no matter how clearly developed, nor ethic, no matter how clearly developed out of logical presuppositions can any longer impart to us the final disclosure, for which we are longing today, that no philosophical cognition can any longer respond to the distresses, despairs, collapses, and transformations that we have lived through. In all these expressions of a changing spirit, however formed, there lives and burns the conviction that today other, more vital certainties are necessary. In place of philosophy there enters the teaching directed to the whole person, in place of the abstract type of human being there enters with his demands and duties the whole, concrete, unique human being.

True, already long before the war there was the poet who announced and presented the principle of form and teaching, and who then preserved this sanctuary through the intellectual-spiritual degeneration of the war. Yet Stefan George stands outside these considerations, because he, proceeding from entirely different foundations, also reaches entirely different results and goals. Here it is only a question of the minds that proceed from thinking, from science, and turn toward it out of a sudden shock and turning back.

A [. . .] highly significant book, which now however is entirely and directly concerned with redemption, *The Star of Redemption,* by Franz Rosenzweig (Verlag J. Kauffmann, Frankfurt a. M.) has already gone beyond the zenith of atheism. Here, certainly, there is not one of those whom Ziegler brands as usurpers and desecrators of the corpse of the dead God, and yet there is at work here one who intuits, a visionary of God rather than a seeker of God. God can in no way die for him; for he remains here fully outside temporal development; he is who he will be: the Eternal One. Time and hour belong to the human being. But it is precisely because of this that the deed of redemption is strictly bound to them; not less unconditionally than where God's living and dying is also drawn into history; here the historical moment of redemption is fixed immovably. For the soul is not absolved [*erlassen*] in any way of the duty of the deification of the world and of self-deification; but this soul knows precisely in its divine task and for its sake that it is not abandoned [*verlassen*] by God but rather loved by Him. Nothing in the universe would be grasped, could be beheld, without this certainty of *God, World,* and *Man*. From the outset every cognition and science is denied that leads to the disavowal of the reality of these three primal words: for they are reality before all knowledge. Thus this book undertakes, out of a deep intuition of the essence of the three original elements and of their movement toward each other, which is disclosed as creation, revelation, and redemption, to construct the entire reality anew and from its own power. Like a great world symphony in a strict triad the universe rises out of the dark of the nothing crossing over through God, world, and man, creation and revelation to the self-illuminating form of redemption. And the last depth of this book is this: that the living, acting human being, whose deed otherwise always broke up or threatened to break up all divine createdness [*Gottgeschaffenheit*], adapts himself here freely into the work of creation and revelation as the perfecter and executor of redemption. Farther still than the others,[1] this book leads as well out of philosophy, stepping almost too brightly, too radiantly, out of our dark reality and yet turning again toward it fully and deeply, by recognizing the redeeming deed for the bringing-about of the eternally present kingdom of God in the living readiness of the soul, in the simple love for the One who is at every time and all the time the nearest.

That which connects all these glowing books of rather different orientation and also still other testimonies of the new spirit as above all the significant, exhorting writings of Rudolf

Pannwitz, is the certainty that not only pure thinking has failed, but yet another essential formation of the German spirit: the organization, that is, the "isms" in both forms. Like a new form of the disclosure of a spiritual certainty, so too, a new form of communal life is being sought. To the conviction that no ethic beyond content, that is, developed out of purely intellectual principles, can give us any longer the essential disclosure, is added the other one, that the true community can be built up only out of the pure living will of the individuals. Instead of pure thinking and research for the attainment of final certainties, the will toward reality enters everywhere; instead of the rigid organizations and parties, the will toward the unique, testifying, and procreative form enters in spirit and life. For all the becoming of form, however, the final sources flow out of that which is no longer calculable, no longer recognizable.

The extreme conclusion to be drawn from this insight that is common to all the vastly different cognitions and confessions, is drawn by Eugen Rosenstock in the tremendous word: "Salvation always comes from where no one expects it, from the cast out [*Verworfenen*], from the impossible." This is the consoling certainty of all these people who turn away from philosophy, from any solution of mere reason, who turn to faith and the realization and final readiness.

One cannot help but be reminded of the woman from the Chinese fairytale, who can only call her husband, whose heart was ripped from his breast by a dragon, back to life again by humiliating herself to the utmost disgrace, by overcoming her frightful disgust, and by swallowing what a mad beggar had spit at her in the marketplace. It sticks in her throat, but just as she, having returned home, bends over the corpse, tears streaming, the horrible, vile thing [*Verworfene*] inside her has turned into the heart of the loved one, which sinks back from her sobbing mouth into his ripped open breast and slowly begins to beat again in it.

It is out of the mood of this fairytale that the seeking of salvation for our world arises. Its heart, too, has been torn from its breast, and only the fully uncalculating and incalculable act of desperate, most personal love, of supreme devotion to the least and lowest up to the overcoming of the disgust of that which is cast out and rejected [*Verworfenen*] can force it back into its empty breast. This is still something different from socialism, at least from everything that it has become. All common work seems to break down in this impenetrably inanimate world; it is dependent only on the unique, personal, animating act of *love*.

Love: this means here a full renunciation of everything that has to do with power in the realm of the soul as well as in the realm of the spirit; for the soul it means its final self-unfolding in active readiness for sacrifice and absolving devotion; for the spirit it means the most difficult renunciation: the sacrifice of that which is farthest away, once so dearly loved, in favor of indefatigable work for that which is most near. The spirit also is no longer to be power; it also has today forfeited the right to roam freely, to understand, to form; it also must acknowledge in active renunciation and self-resignation the destroyed foundations of life and operate in calm, decisive work for that which today is necessary.

That is why it is no accident that among the people turned toward the future there are wide circles that profess a *Christianity* which is renewed from within. And among them again it is our entire community, although held together by no organization, in which today the faith is alive, which actually is more a will that precisely Germany, as the land whose outer existence today is completely broken, should be called as the first to find the way to a Christian life animated from within; because, just in the brokenness of the "pagan," of the national world of power, there lies the indispensable precondition for becoming, of a world standing under the sign of the cross, that is, of the return.

Whether now, however, the way to the re-formation stands under the sign of the cross or under the pagan sign of self-deification, or that of the messianic dream of the redemption that sublates the world: wherever the course of pure thought, of abstract cognition is abandoned, we find today the same building forces at work. By way of the most horrible detour through the outside we have arrived in the highest of our people in the inside again: at an inwardness, however, which is a coming in and turning around. For now it is determined never again to abandon and surrender the outside, but rather to give itself to it consciously in painful love and actively for its transformation.

5

New Philosophy

HANS EHRENBERG

It was a decade ago when, among the disciples of the oldest
of all sciences, philosophy, there was a small group of novices
who courageously professed their allegiance to Hegel—a confession that, at that time, still cost his adherents their profes-
sional reputation, until the Nestor of philosophy of that time,
Wilhelm Windelband, legitimized the young people with his
Heidelberg lecture on "the renewal of Hegelianism."

A decade and more has passed. Today the adherence to
Hegel no longer costs anyone his academic prospects. And yet
that group has become smaller, rather than larger. That fleet-
ing second spring of Hegelianism was important all the same.
For as long as the present philosophers played around only in
the outer court of (Hegel's) absolute idealism, with Kant,
Fichte, the early Schelling—for that length of time the secret

From *Die Frankfurter Zeitung,* 29 December, 1921.

of their being epigones was kept. Hence also the shying away from Hegel; conversely the inclination toward him on the part of those who had renounced the status of epigone, philosophical or otherwise. For, following him, copied thought could no longer conceal itself behind creativity. Thanks to neo-Hegelianism, a separation took place between these two, but just this separation cost him his own life. As for a bee that may sting once, but then must lose its life, so it was for him.

But how had that odd situation arisen, in which university-philosophy believed it could limit itself to the stretch of the road "from Kant to Hegel"? To this enclave within the mighty history of thought three thousand years in the making! How above all could one stop with Hegel, that is to say, before him. Only through a boundless contempt, borne by academic presumption, for the names Schopenhauer and Nietzsche, and through the silencing of the philosophy of the really mature Schelling!

The young people of that small group soon had to undergo this experience. If they had been daring enough to profess their allegiance to Hegel, why should they be too timid now to liberate themselves again from Hegel? The thanks of the initiates is even then, by no means, withheld from the former master. But only to become a Hegel with different premises, a different systematics, perhaps even an opposite tendency and yet just a "Hegel redivivus"—against which the aging Schelling, under unspeakable burdens, had fought life long—for this that group was not only too proud, but also too much alive!

The decision came about in this movement, not as a result of a systematic train of thought, but much more from the philosophizing one himself. He remained, however, an insoluble foreign body in the nitric acid of all his systematics. Nietzsche's tragic image of life also left behind an effect that was formative, not tragic. "The philosopher!" the unsolved problem of all philosophy "of the old kind"—unsolved, because never posed—"hence" unknown also to the academic philosophy of the present.

Isn't the philosopher, then, an intellectual [*geistig*] activist? Not a leader or misleader? Not a prophet or a will-o'-the-wisp? Not a spiritual healer or a quack? Finally considered in himself: not one whose thinking derives from torment or from blessings?! And should he alone in the world not be fully responsible for himself: for what he himself does and leaves undone? Under such questions writhes the soul of the one who philosophizes, but it was only until the sower death plowed up the soil in such a way that the germinating little plants could grow.

We stand today before such a plant grown to the size of a full trunk in Franz Rosenzweig's *The Star of Redemption* (F. Kaufmann, Frankfurt, 1921). The author made himself known in the scholarly world through his two-volume work *Hegel and the State,* a historical work of great scope, but entirely in the scientific spirit. The new work is of a different kind. It hardly exists within the same epoch, even though it may partly owe its origin to that state of affairs which, with the end of the war, released forces in some people that had long been leashed, even as it shackled forces in others that for a long time had been able to operate freely.

The recapitulation of the work runs up against difficulties, because it does not, in the manner of the philosophies of the old kind, want to "explain," and for this reason it cannot be characterized by any "Ism." In truth, philosophy has explained reality as soon as it—has narrated it. This is already what the older Schelling meant when he opposed to the negative philosophy of Hegel the positive philosophy of revelation. For the language of facts is harder than any other language. Philosophy, for this reason, is overall just as unnameable as the reality of life and of the eternal facts. In the tides of creation, revelation, and redemption the cycle of facts takes its course—of all facts, not by any chance only the cycle of religious ones. Isolation becomes impossible. Division no longer threatens the inherently indivisible fullness of existence. Thinking sees itself liberated from abstract points of view, and thereupon no longer takes refuge in mysticism or in the pietism of faith that is hostile to knowledge. In the framework of the whole each person finds himself again—even with the Ism that is his own; yet, as in life, each individual disappears in the whole, and so too fares his Ism; it goes under in the whole, the "philosophical narrative" triumphs over all points of view and circles round the course of life, be it that of the individual, be it that of the cosmos.

Arrangement and conceptuality are also in the story. Construction in regard to the whole and logic in regard to detail permeate the book. The thread of the story unwinds unbroken, and not only makes the heart content but also satisfies the legitimate claims of reason. One can speak only negatively of a point of view; for the turn against idealism is expressed harshly, with a healthy clarity, and yet each avoids even the smallest concession to the hazy philosophies of life. If philosophy here turns away from the tyranny of the spirit, it does not by this enter the shadowy and misty fields of emotion, but rather the brightly sunlit land of the soul. A philosophy whose innermost core is called *soul* and that extends the measures of the soul also throughout the spiritual domains, such a philosophy surely can no longer be idealistic. It is system in the sense of the whole of life, not in the sense of a logistical systematic. It is universal, not universalistic (as for instance Spengler), and refined in the most beautiful sense: the first philosophy that is not written only for men.

And if everyone finds himself in it, then he does not come away from the book without bending down and repenting, without having been changed and transformed; the secret of the soul is the manifest strength from which the perceptions of this book are derived. This secret, however, is called: *God*. The new philosophy knows nothing anymore except the miracle of revelation of the soul. Out of this, philosophy lets itself be offered again the free use of reason, even of the intellect [*Intellekt*]. And thus out of faith comes knowledge! The striving for knowledge finds only fragments if it sets out to fathom the world without the strength of the secret of faith; what it gets then are only elements, and what it can assemble out of the elements is only the loose structure of the prehistorical world [*Vorwelt*], the past of the human race as it is preserved for us in the antiquity of Asia and Europe. This gives the first part of the book. However, the elements are assembled in pairs into the real structure; that which lay side by side loose and not joined together, becomes indissolubly linked in "renewal spanning all times," connected to and consolidated as the spiritual structure of the soul; the forces fall into place, order permeates a whole, and life streams without interruption through the closed circle of existence. There no part is separated, loving and being loved in return hold the unwieldy parts together in an eternal bond. This is the second part consisting of creation, revelation, and redemption. But as the elements were there before the present of the spiritual house [*Geisteshaus*] of the soul was built, so now the form of the future emerges out of the house, in the communities of eternal life that grow toward God, in the church and in the synagogue—as the third part. In past, present, and future the circle of the whole becomes complete. No one who has once entered this circle can step outside it without being marked.

Even the disciplines of the old kind of philosophy come into their own, so that in this sense the designation philosophical system, even though it is not used by the author, would be justified. Yet the disciplines are not found self-contained, rather they are interwoven through the course of the story like several red threads. So, for instance, aesthetics surfaces in almost every chapter. This will perhaps not be to everyone's liking, but at least it is a fruitful way of freeing philosophy finally, for once, from the constraints of a systematic stemming from the beginnings of philosophy, without thereby lapsing into the empty mishmash of the modern philosophies of life.

Here and there the book presents great difficulties. Nevertheless it makes the reader—into a listener; and it is easier to keep listening than to read further. It is much too full of music not to stir in us sooner or later the echo of a melody that then resounds until the melody of the book comes to an end. So it offers us the fullness of life, contained in the container of thought. Content and form are in harmony. Therefore a fragrance wafts from it as from a tree in full bloom, and yet this fragrance does not intoxicate. True, it cannot be called fruit;

a recognizable school will hardly come of it. Yet it will have an effect in the way a living person has an effect, atmospheric and penetrating, and will steal into the heart like everything that stems from the heart and has been nourished with the blood of love.

Where there is light, there is also shade. Where the soul reigns so very much, there *nature* and *spirit* come up short. Above all, the absence of a philosophy of nature is surprising; only a few of its building blocks are provided. And even within the philosophy of spirit one can notice many great gaps: the logic that Rosenzweig calls to new life by means of a profound philosophy of language, inserted between mathematics and liturgy, does not culminate in a theory of science, and the ethics is too much absorbed through the conversation of the soul in faith, love, and hope. Art and politics are marked out most completely. And yet the philosophical value of the book will be more and more concentrated in the parts that would have to be designated, with an old word, as metaphysical. Here the thought has poured out a full cornucopia of concepts, blessèd concepts. Compared to them the concepts of the pres-ent-day philosophers look like dead bones.

With this work philosophy stands already inside the gate to a new time. Refuted are the false modesty and resignation on which many a contemporary prides himself. And even theol-ogy wins a new field and new faces. Philosophy and theology are, after all, inseparably connected: they both belong to the realm of the soul. To be sure, the one looks to the world, the other towards God, and thus they will never completely co-incide with one another, and yet only the direction of their gaze is different; apart from that they are more and more alike and with time reveal themselves to be twins, sons of the same father. They have known this for a long time; and it was only that they didn't want to admit it to each other just yet. Then they even separated from each other; but it was only an apparent separation, for what they sent out under their names were only shadows, which at times they detached from themselves. And now the time is ripe. That is the keynote to which today that little group about which we spoke at the beginning has been tuned. What the mystical orientation sought, but did not attain, that is herewith won.

The author's confession, moreover, goes toward Judaism. No religion, after all, is quite so confined to the land of the soul as this one. None was summoned so strongly to liberate the land of the soul from those who had occupied it, from the abstract forms of a spirit without a soul. True, Christian sentiment is not likely to be satisfied with the third part—where the author describes the individual religions and where he also attempts an appreciation of Christianity, yet even this is stimulating. Nevertheless, I am connecting also the deficiencies of the book mentioned above with the Jewish confession; that nature and spirit come up short must have a connection with Judaism. As for the rest, the most lofty parts of the book, seen from the vantage of faith, as well stand beyond Judaism and Christianity, in that holy space that is common to them both.

The only thing that I regret about the book—inasmuch as the faults mentioned above cannot really detract from it—is the unnecessary last word with which the author, who surely does not need to speak in this way, concludes, paying tribute to our times by suddenly joining in the call: "*from philosophy to life.*"

The secret of life is first of all like a bud. Most people know it only in this state of development; others can also pluck the fruit into which the bud transforms itself in the end, but only to a few chosen ones is it granted to gaze upon the blossom in the moment of its fullest splendor. The glance of such a one looks deeply into the secret of existence, all the way down to its ground, and yet he beholds it still surrounded by the protecting leaves of the calyx, and thus he may unveil the secret and yet will not desecrate it. In the one to whom this is granted, faith and love are in intimate harmony: God gave him more than only talents and genius. New epochs and new series of works can take their point of departure only from such individuals.

6

The Star of Redemption

RUDOLF HALLO

It has been about a year since a book by Franz Rosenzweig was reviewed in this newspaper—by Hans Hess—for the first time. At that time it was a philosophic-historical one: *Hegel and the State*.[1] That book stems from 1913, and in its foreword one reads that in 1920 it could at best still have been published, but no longer written. In the book under discussion today, the author has unveiled his human face before us; the philosophy that veils has stepped down (not sunk down) from its position of reigning to one of serving. For in *The Star of Redemption* its entire range fills only just the first of three books. *In Philosophos*[2] turns out to be a difficult treatise (though no more difficult than one by Keyserling or Steiner) that opposes to the idealist philosophy that had separated spirit from body, the *human*

From *Casseler Tageblatt,* no. 173, 21 April 1921. Note: passages marked by an asterisk appear only in the typescript version of the review, in the collection of the Leo Baeck Institute, New York City.

being, who scoffs at just that separation into spirit and body in his fear of death (this is to be taken quite literally). He is the constant refuter of the philosophy that only seemingly liberates. He, the human being, is also the one to whom things can happen in his Being-here [*Da-Sein*], that is, in his singularity, not-being-there [*Nicht-dort-Sein*], in his "discrete" essence, [things] that connect him with the other, be it the other human being, be it the Creator; that build bridges from the Here to the There, a bridge building that remains inexplicable from the point of view of the discrete essence, that is, remains *miraculous.* Therefore, the second book turns out to be *In Theologos,*[3] because they want to deny the miracle and get rid of it altogether. What must follow is clear to anyone with understanding, for to the Being-here there necessarily belongs the Being-now, that is, the Not-being-yesterday but also Not-being-tomorrow. Thus, the third book turns out to be *In Tyrannos,*[4] who are those who think they can force the kingdom of heaven to come, and who forget that they are only *today* and not at the end of the days (although the today can become the end of the days). Naturally, then, the third book is historical and richly metaphorical.

These are the three stations. One will say: What is different here than elsewhere? Does it not remain philosophy, a product of thought, something spiritual? *No.* For the path is not determined by thought, neither its beginning (cognition), nor its middle (experience), nor its end (event), but rather shown, by day and manifestly in the Jew. Hence his uniqueness, for he does not separate body from spirit, but rather suffers for the sake of his pride and is proud of his suffering; suffering, however, is a distinguishing mark of the body, as pride is the mark of the spirit. [In this, his opposition to the philosophical man who claims to have overcome the suffering of his body through the spirit, and likewise the opposition to the natural man who suffers in spite of all spirit under the painful mortality of his body, becomes clear.★] Hence his disapora, his *Galut,* for only in this way is he here and there. Hence, according to the expression of the nations, the "eternal" Jew, for only thus is he yesterday and today and—*still* tomorrow. [But in order to be chosen, to be able to be here and there, still to exist now and earlier and later, the Jew needs the non-Jew.★] It is almost the greatest feature of this great book, that the pre-Christian pagans just like the Christians are understood as necessary. This alone already would move the book into the ranks of the most important ones. That this apology, or, better put, this laying of the foundation of Christianity, does not follow more broadly and more assuredly, is unfortunately the weakness of the book. But here is where the Jewish writer (generally speaking) seems to reach his limits. *Up to* these limits *everything* has been said.

7

The Star of Redemption

EDUARD STRAUSS

European philosophy may confidently be equated with Idealism; at any rate, in it its work of more than a thousand years most purely took effect. Idealism "from Ionia to Jena," from Parmenides to Hegel, reveals the meaning of the entire philosophical endeavor: to think the All, to find unity *in* thinking and *out of* thinking. To encompass entirely the whole of being, the multiplicity of everything real, must be the final goal of philosophy. Its end is plainly signified, its goal reached, when it succeeds as well in constructing even its own history in the form of the all-encompassing system. This is what Hegel's system actually accomplished. It is only strange, that philosophizing did not now really cease. Strange that, precisely at the moment of this final event, a man stepped up, with all the gestures of rage, even despair, and transformed the festive cere-

From *Das neue Deutschland,* ed. Dr. Adolf Grabowsky. 10. Jahr, Heft 13/14. April-Doppelheft 1922, 208–11.

mony of the completion into a funeral ceremony: this man was Arthur Schopenhauer. He explained bluntly that the whole work of philosophical thinking, the whole attempt to think the All, was led on by death and led away from life. But after all what a man wanted was to get free of death, and it was precisely this that philosophy had promised him; now he sees that one has tried to deceive him cruelly about an incontrovertible fact by means of a deceptive sentence: death is nothing [*Nichts*]—so taught philosophy. But death *is,* is very real, is again and again—something.

Schopenhauer's thinking—for the first time—is decisively determined by the entirely personal question concerning the worth of the world and of life. This philosopher "after all philosophy" prefers to shatter the world into ruins rather than to let his question be disputed away. After Schopenhauer comes Nietzsche: still more precipitously, still more inexorably in him the human being rises up above his highest peak thus far, the philosophical thinking-the-All, and plunges down. This plunge and that question could never remain episodes and did not remain so. With ever renewed force the questioning of the living actualities confronts at this time the ever further reading, laborious, philosophic-scientific activity: before the closed system of ethics, the regulation of our human life, there stands the living human being; before the indomitable edifice of logic, the mastery of our thinking, there stands the real content of the world; before the magic palace of our ideals, piled up overnight by subservient demons out of the nothing—the living [*leibhaft*] God: these three can no longer be left aside in thinking. Imperiously they demand their right.

A work that, not prematurely and not too late—at *its* time

and hence at the right time—entered the present generation, undertakes to go through the threefold problematic, looks in the face of that which exists, and offers a strong and great vision. Franz Rosenzweig has, with full awareness, placed his *Star of Redemption* (Frankfurt a.M. 1920, J. Kauffmann) there where thinking must build further—No: must build anew, unless again and yet again a plunge into the bottomless is to follow further attempts; he turns away from idealism: but he does not turn now to any new or—fundamentally—old "ism," but rather he seizes—reality. Rosenzweig takes his point of departure not from the "nothing" of idealism but from the nothing that is "something." And he finds three "nothings" [*Nichtse*] which are three "somethings" [*Etwasse*]: "the elements" God, world, man. With their triad they provide the groundplan of the whole edifice. They form the content of what the pagan world—what Greece, India, China lived and still live: God— hidden in his metaphysical Being; the world—locked in its metalogical meaning; man—mute and solitary in his metaethical self. This is what remains of the "possibility to know the all": this "All" bursts into three pieces. Here is the point at which Rosenzweig's work distinguishes itself from what philosophers undertook up to now: they proceeded from the "All," claimed it to be thinkable, and made it thinkable for so long, until graspable reality was eternally and without the possibility of mediation confronted with a nameless "essence," and until the thinking human being himself—the two great names of our time have shown it—plunged headlong into the abyss of the world or of the spirit that yawns between: *the* nothing [*Nichts*]—which is that abyss.

Rosenzweig summoned up the courage to proceed from

the *pieces* and not only to make use of the philosophical instrument for construction. He knows from the earliest beginning of his way that the real All does not lie behind him, but can appear in full totality only at the end. Thus he does not begin with the question: "What is truth?" or "How do I attain it?" Nor at the beginning does he pursue that which philosophy sees as absolutely necessary: a theory of knowledge. The theory of truth and truth itself—are at the end.

First of all, the living relationship between the "elements," and in fact out of them themselves, must be set, so that the course emerges that is sketched in the sky of the world-day. The image of the "star" is not mere image: it is a real simile. The elements, as they come to be, stand beside one another; they do not submit to any order. They are only forced by the "theological" concepts creation, revelation, redemption into a fixed relationship with each other and into the bound course. If Rosenzweig directs the introduction of the first part against the *philosophers,* then that of the second goes against the *theologians.*

In a sharply outlined image of the problem history it is shown how today, finally, philosophy is capable of placing the miracle, the favorite child of faith, in the lap of theology. Through the miraculous experience of revelation the secret of creation is unsealed. The mute human being, who is only creature, steps out of taciturnity when God lovingly draws nearer to him and opens his mouth for the revealing answer, into the day of the ever renewed world: with it he grows toward the perfection of all creation. In the triple time of creation—revelation—redemption, which are not as it were "categories of thought," but form a single, unique, cooperating event with a real beginning and a real ending, the foundation of things, the birth of the soul, the future of the kingdom of God in formed and forming relationship, now step toward each other in a triply repeated simile of human and of divine love.

The transition from the first to the second part led from secret to miracle. Stepping over the threshold of the second part we enter the sphere of illumination. Now the simile of the title is fulfilled: fire, rays, and the form of the star become visible. In the fire the eternal life glows; the rays flash on the eternal path; the star itself, however, is the eternal truth. It is not that the truth is God, as Idealism wants it, but rather that God is the truth: He is not "all in all" but above the world redeemed for the All—the Lord.

But, since the kingdom of perfection, of omnipotence, is one of total nonviolence, the final Introduction may turn against the *tyrants,* by dealing with the greatest possibility—that is to say with the possibility of obtaining the kingdom by prayer. But the kingdom, lying far distant from all the goals of progress of Idealism, which, on acount of their being infinite do not materialize *even* in eternity, will unite all reality in the "we," will give life to all that there is. The last miracle will be greater than the first. In redemption, creation is per-fected [*voll-endet*].

The eternal life and the eternal way: in these two signs Jew and Christian part ways. Out of the last and highest vision the gate leads into *life.* With a full great final harmony this work, which opened with the words "from death," ends.

It cannot be my task to detail the whole abundance housed in this edifice and traced here only roughly in its plan. Here there is really a book, formed out of a single vision and *constructed* in unconditional symmetry, that carries out the triple time of its parts down to the smallest detail. It not only delivers what is announced as the philosophical and theological subjects in the titles of its three parts and of its nine books, and which is worked out in a new and splendidly conveyed method, out of the mathematical symbol and out of the meaning of language. Precisely the trusting use of language is highly significant here: for it, the miraculous instrument of revelation and God's real first gift to human beings, comes decisively into its own inherent right in the face of all idealistic and skeptical criticism. After the "artificial" sign language of the pre-world it opens its mouth, building the bridge from what is secret to what is revealed. Its binding word leads up from the human being to redeemed humanity, until on the seventh day in the silence of perfection—the farthest stretched antithesis to the speechlessness of the primal beginning—worshipping movement and glance of the eye are likewise no longer in need of it.

Throughout all the books the essence of the arts, in which creation, revelation, redemption really become mere categories in order to end in an apotheosis of the applied—"churchly"—art that overcomes the idealistic formalism of "pure" aesthetics, is pursued in the form of a necessary episode. The theory of state as well as society similarly extends, in a peculiar interweaving with anti- and metapolitical motives, throughout the entire work.

The first part takes its "facts" from the West and the East of the ancient world; the theology of the second part finds its counterexample in each case in Islam; the holy festival year of the Jew and that of the Christian demonstrates the life-contents of the eternal superworld (this also is significant—"super*world*," and no longer "super*man*" is discussed here!), and shows how Jew and Christian pray for the kingdom of God. With the exception of this one, there is no single "new concept" to be found in Rosenzweig's work—except perhaps for this one. His method puts into his hands always and without the aid of new and foreign words the realities of this existence of ours and *our* entirely graspable humanity that is given to each of us. Again and again everything that is only probable is thrust aside until the truth remains and no appearance is valid any longer.

Such a work could only be conceived and written out of a sensitivity to life that contains wholeness in its deepest depth, a sensitivity to life that from the very beginning has been marked by eternity and must have received its determining impulse through revelation: only such a sensitivity to life was able to set into this dark hour of the world with the certainty of a "Truly, I say to you," this fully complete, fully brightly and clearly lived-through work. This sensitivity to *life* must at the same time be a sensitivity to *world*. Is there a "living being" [*Lebewesen*] who in its being, in all and everything that was and is its own, begetting from generation to generation, bears eternity as a distinctive mark? Rosenzweig wrote his book out of his *Jewish* consciousness of eternity. What he says about Jewish being carries nothing at all defensive in it, nor is it achieved by philosophizing—he gives a "philosophy of Judaism" as little as he does a philosophy of Christianity. Jew and Christian stand here in their entire, holy, divinely determined reality: the Christian, eternally being, in his existence outside the epochs of history anticipating redemption; the Jew eternally young, spreading revelation over all creation on the way through world history. The Christian—the messenger; the Jew eternally confirming the messenger and yet constituting an eternal contradiction to him until the day when time breaks up, when all paganism sinks down and each portion in the truth harmonizes in a single Truly [*Wahrlich*].— Really this book speaks for all and to all, and yet is the worldbook of a *Jew*. Books whose creators stand under revelation, if they are great—and this one is great—have one characteristic: they did not grow but are built. And they are always "penultimate" books, for the last and at the same time first "book" of the Jews, that is only—built, but not by human hands—the book of revelation itself. The Jew is always purest and greatest when he explains this world of his, the Holy Scripture. This is just as much the case with Rosenzweig as in the last work of his revered master Hermann Cohen—and perhaps also Rosenzweig's method, to let language itself "speak," has here its deepest subconscious root.

[. . .]

Rosenzweig's *Star of Redemption* does not shine forth in the red-hot flame of mysticism, but rather in the white light of revelation—sharply and rigorously he opposes this searching turning of his contemporaries toward the formless East.—The Western consciousness appears today to be released from Jewish-Christian revelation; without support between the rooted, primal mysticism and the airy tree-top of the free spirit, it turns back now toward the root. The top of the thousand-year-old tree no longer has any fruit to offer: in spite of all horticultural efforts, the noble fruit of idealism does not ripen a second time around Kant. A rigorous science of philosophy works further—and this likewise points in its strongest thinkers—precisely with its rigor that advances matters and its analysis of meaning that comprehends language—beyond itself into the direction that Rosenzweig's book takes.

Mauthner's and Spengler's books perhaps will grow antiquated and will lead a library life of science as signs of this cultural epoch; in this way already Schopenhauer and Nietzsche can *not* grow antiquated, for they are begotten [*gezeugt*] out of something living and give testimony [*zeugen*] to something living. Rosenzweig's book—entire expositions, the style, much of it or little, may pay tribute to the time—will not become *as* antiquated as those books, but—also will not remain alive *in* such a "pagan" way as the individualities, Schopenhauer and Nietzsche. For it draws its strength not out of a mystical-individual feeling of life, but out of the community's feeling of life that "can never express the 'we' of its oneness without hearing along with it in its innermost being the complementary 'are eternal.'"

Such thinking stands before God full of humility: It animates life actually and in truth. The life to which it testifies, this eternal life, will go on procreating/bearing witness.

I said that the Western consciousness is "released" from revelation. Here for the first time its drink, seemingly so insipid and stale since Fichte's *Versuch einer Kritik aller Offenbarung,* (Essay toward a critique of all revelation), is offered again to the one who thirsts. Again the root and the treetop of life appear joined through living sap that courses through the trunk. Perhaps—my confidence says: Surely—new fruit is ripening.

8

Franz Rosenzweig
The Star of Redemption (A Review)

MARGARETE SUSMAN

A name is not sound and smoke, it is word and fire. The
name must be named and professed: I believe in it.
— Franz Rosenzweig

This book comes, self-consciously, at a great turning point, a
time of decay, of the degeneration of the philosophy of pure
thought that has dominated the Western world from Parmenides to Hegel. At this moment, when life and death enter the center of consciousness with their final, decisive
questions, we can see that the philosophy of pure thought has
no strength left to resolve life and redeem us from death.

From *Der Jude* 7 (1923), 457–64, trans. Joachim Neugroschel, in
Arthur A. Cohen, *The Jew: Essays from Martin Buber's Journal,* Der
Jude, *1916–1928* (Tuscaloosa: Univ. of Alabama Press, 1980), 276–85.

In Hegel's system, philosophy's culmination—the unity and universality of knowledge enclosing everything, even God—the philosophy of pure thought found its end. "If from this peak we are to take another step without plunging into the abyss, we must first shift the foundations and bring forth a new concept of philosophy" [2:22].

And it *was* brought forth. The moment a thinker first shifted the problem of his own person, his personal self, to the center of comprehension, something uncomprehended, incomprehensible, unthinkable outside of the thinkable became visible. The moment Schopenhauer first asked the question about the worth or worthlessness of a man's life, for his own person, rather than about the essence of the world, like all prior thinkers; the moment Kierkegaard introduced the deep consciousness of personal sin and personal redemption, a consciousness seeking its personal solution far from the essence of the world; the moment Nietzsche, last but not least, presented the now ineradicable "fearful and demanding image of the unconditional allegiance of the soul to the mind" [1:15]—at that world-historic moment, when, at the midpoint of living and thinking, the human individual became a visible, self-centered, fully alone, otherworldly human individuality, living out of its own responsibility, dying for itself alone—at that moment, the sphere of the all-embracing one and conceivable universe was burst. "An enclosed unity had rebelled and, by sheer obstinacy, obtained its withdrawal" [1:18].

And it was only now, with the entrance of this ungraspable, unthinkable into the innermost sphere of human problems, that life and death were suddenly here in their full, shattering reality, demanding their solution. Life in all its depth, solitarily rooted in the abyss of the self; death in all its horrific factuality—not as death *per se,* such as previous philosophy had known it, but as the countless deaths of innumerable individuals, dying by and for themselves. It is now a matter of embracing this life, isolated and boundless in its plurality—it is a matter of overcoming the real and true death of the individual. For death had always been the deeply frightening enigma driving against all philosophy, and yet no philosophy had ever been able to overcome it, precisely because each philosophy understood it only as an abstract death, which it snuffed out in its one existing universe. "For indeed, a universe could not die and nothing would die in the universe, only the particular can die, and all dying is lonesome" [1:8].

The one-dimensional form of the system, a form that was scientific only on the assumption of an objective world and a single and general thinking, crumbled before the wealth of overflowing individual life. But the first consequence of that plurality of thinker-individualities, growing aware of themselves, more lonesome, living out of themselves, was a tremendous peril for all philosophy: there *was* henceforth to be no more philosophy—merely philosophies, ideologies, self-contained, isolated standpoints: a complete relativism of knowledge. Every thinker, every cognizant individual now carried about his own space, time, and truth.

But just as the full, burning desire for overcoming death was first kindled by a fully experienced, lonesome, real death (a victory different from anything that the philosophy of pure thinking had ever known), so too this utmost, perfect relativism, this immensely isolating subjectivity of knowledge, kindled the full, the innermost desire for overcoming death in a real, collective truth, which is also an experienced and a lived collectivity of existence, in which all separated selves find and redeem themselves.

This will, this yearning of present-day time, gave birth to Franz Rosenzweig's book *The Star of Redemption*—the will to grasp life and death in their living, concrete plurality, as it emerges only from post-Hegelian philosophy, and to overcome life and death in their true shape by means of a spreading, universal truth. In this will to grasp all life in its full breadth, height, and depth, the book declares war to the blood against the one-dimensional idealism of all ages, that mortal foe of all living wholeness, and from that yearning, the book embraces all powers of life as forces of immediate revelation. And from the yearning as well for redemption in a universal truth, the book shifts its demand in accordance with its overall foundations, urging toward a fully changed form of cognition: to knowledge out of the revelations of life itself. Thus life and truth roar for it into a vast chord; it is not a matter of grasping the truth of thinking, after all—but of unveiling the countenance of *living* truth out of life and death and overcoming both by means of an everlasting brilliance.

This is the only possible way of understanding this book: as the will to climb down to the origins and there draw immediate life for the still unshaped elements of being; as the will to see and to speak clearly the outlines of all living things in the full, burning light of day; and as the will to ascend to the stars and expose pure eternity in its place again—and thus exhibit all the deepest and highest things of life in their steady places below and above man—so that the clearly viewed order will make directly visible to man his eternal meaning and, thereby, the redemption through truth itself.

The one thinkable universe does not surround us immediately: this certitude comes first. Before knowing and thinking, we find realities in and around us. Hence, that one universe is not the prerequisite for our cognition—these realities are the prerequisite. Just as the one universe is not the prerequisite to our thinking, so too, the lack of a prerequisite for our thinking is not the mere void. Instead, countless disparate, separate "voids," one for each problem, precede our cognition. Every particular knowledge begins with the void of the as-yet-unthought reality underlying it, preceding it as a dark, struggling life-will to cognition. The void is grasped as the place where this special problem dawns, as "the visual place of the beginning of our knowledge."

For everything, after all, became different for cognition when the one thinkable universe was no longer the all-embracing whole. Not only was the universe smashed into many particular subjects of cognition, but the subject of the thinker, having forced its retreat from thinkableness necessarily finds itself confronted by a different world from the thinkable one that heretofore included the thinker. With that retreat, the universe was also abandoned by that which hitherto, as the point of utmost unity of subject and object, inwardness and world, held the universe together: God. Thus the thinker no longer faces that thinkable universe but rather a trinity of independent realities, into which the universe has crumbled, and each of which confronts him as a perfectly unthinkable, self-enclosed, and sealed whole, the trinity of God, world, and man. None of these three realities has previously been known, no, or even seen in this self-dependence, this inmost isolation that mocks any common precondition. Each of these three must first be sought out in its own "void," must be pulled into the light of cognition and utterance from the darkness of all preconditional life. For that is one and the same: the Word, discourse, is also revelation. The fact that the mute, primal words, which precede all speech, are spoken is the same as the process by which reality becomes visible. And, from the mute night of their voids, the three last great primal beings slowly ascend. In a deep, wondrous view of their being, they unravel more and more clearly from the mystery of their voids, and the sought-for "everlastingness, not needful of thought in order to exist," is disclosed to us. Still directionless, still mute, still fully self-enclosed, they arise from the hush of preconscious life, exist for themselves in towering loneliness: the metaphysical God, the metalogical world, the metaethical man. Disconnected, unrelated to one another, they are pure in their being, unfolded from their innermost ardent core, pure products of the seeing spirit. Each sets itself up monastically as the whole. "We have the parts in hand, we have truly smashed the universe." What can be done so that they shall not remain parts, mere disintegrating elements of life? How shall the mutually alienated elements combine anew, become reality again, the reality we know them to be—the truly existing All?

There are many ways in which they could move in order to come together again, just as there have been many interpretations of God, the world, man, and their mutual relationship—and yet, in this orgiastic chaos of possibilities, this veritable

Walpurgisnacht of confusedly whirling shapes, only one can be the true, the real. Only movement out of themselves toward one another can combine the elements into the meaningful togetherness that constitutes our reality. What is that one path, the only one matching their inmost being, which, in and out of itself, overcomes the elementary internal mangling of reality?

The answer to this question exposes the full depth of the abyss separating this philosophy from previous modes of cognition. No thinking can achieve the eternally valid fusion. Only reality itself achieved it and continues to achieve it. From the night of preconscious being, in which we found each element by itself, within the realm of wellsprings, which is their realm, we are carried upward in the full light of day by the only river in which we find the elements in their unique and eternally valid fusion: History. History, considered not in its mere, extant factuality, but history as a specific meaningful structure, a unique development, "the one river of world-time, which from world-morning through world-noon to world-evening brings together what was flung apart into the darkness of the Something: the elements of the All, in the one world-day of the Lord."

"In the one world-day of the Lord"—such language is no longer that of philosophy. And together with the question of the new fusion of the elements of the All, which had been flung apart in the breath of the full reality of life, we once again hear that first question: Given the collapse of philosophy into countless subjective viewpoints, how can truth be possible? Is not the loss in richness of life that the objective systems of idealism suffered in reality more than made up for by the greater objectivity of cognition of truth? Must not this lack—in regard to subjectivity of standpoints—be replaced by an even greater one, that of renouncing any possibility of objective truth?

Rosenzweig sees the full scope of the danger. But in seeing it, he has already found the path to overcoming it—a path none other than the one that leads the rigid, disintegrated elements back to the living reality. The same path leads to both reality and truth. Most likely, this turn, despite total rethinking, will still appear strange and surprising—but only to him who does not reexperience the deeply felt ascendancy of the living person to grasp meaning over the power of pure thought.

Alongside the abyss to which philosophy of knowledge had led, another abyss opened, and another failure became clear: the failure of theology, which likewise had come to the end of its road. Just as philosophy threatened to fall apart into individual, disconnected standpoints and just as it thereby seemed compelled to forego objective truth, so theology also was threatened with having the foundation of truth erode beneath it when it deprived itself of its hitherto most solid pillar, the understanding of revelation as a miracle, and had replaced once and for all established truth more and more completely with mere experience. Rosenzweig realized that the one specific for both philosophy and theology was for each to help the other since each possesses what the other lacks. After all, both philosophy and theology have the same content: life from its most modest foundations to redemption—except that for theology revelation *is,* whereas philosophy must prove the merest precondition of revelation, that is, its cognitive basis. Philosophy, as the theologian understands it, becomes the prophecy of revelation, the Old Testament of theology. By supplying the grounds for revelation (and thereby precisely what theology has lost) philosophy becomes the new *auctoritas* of theology, restoring to revelation its lost miraculousness by prophesying revelation and thereby disclosing its superhistorical truth. Philosophy is intended to bring subjective cognition to theology and theology the great objective truth to philosophy, the objective truth that it lacked and that will henceforth be justified by philosophy itself. For the bridge from "deaf and blind selfness to the most radiant objectivity of reason" is built only by the theological concept of revelation. From now on every philosopher must be a theologian, that is, must have faith, and every theologian must be a philosopher, that is, must seek cognition; they must join forces to achieve the interpretation of Being, the one true, living, and whole interpretation. And just as their union overcomes the subjectivity of the philosophy of viewpoints, so, too, their certitude overcomes the particularization of the elements of the All— for now they enter, have entered into the great torrent of the historical process of salvation and are united into the All in a world-day of the Lord.

Their path is also thereby unequivocally determined. The way of brightness lights up in the dark heaven of eternity, the way described by the star of redemption, which is heaven itself. In a rigorous triple form, in the shape of the double three-pointed star, the new All emerges before us from the motion of the primal elements toward one another from the innermost essence of the star shape—and the new All that results is a tremendous interpretation of the meaning of the world, of the soul, of God in a living relationship: creation, revelation, redemption. These are the three great eternal pathways, at whose final points, God, the world, and man achieve living contact. Only the concept of creation can achieve what had demolished the great universal concept of idealism: the interpretation of the phenomenon of constantly renewed life, of the living, torrential abundance of forms, of the spiritual permanence of the wholly extraspiritual, thoroughly unthinkable Being; and at the same time, the interpretation of the essence of God, which arises over the darkness of the everlasting world of old as an eternally renewing creative will, developing that old world into a flowering world of light, the world of formed creation. Likewise, revelation alone can determine how man comes into the world, how he is freed from the deaf and blind soul into the soul beloved by God, a soul that carries the love it received back to creation and thereby returns creation back to God. Freed only by God's love, it can betake itself to the last of the three great pathways, which leads from man by way of creation back to God.

Redemption is thereby put into the hands of man. Just as the world completes itself in creation, so too, man, the self, is completed in the sacred, in the servant of God. Yet the final word of redemption is spoken by God. For what shall come is the Kingdom: redemption, the self-perfection of God. "God becomes in redemption that which the frivolity of human thought has always and everywhere sought, everywhere claimed and yet nowhere found, because it could not be found anywhere, for it did not yet exist: All and One."

Here the All, the one and All, becomes visible—but only visible. It has not yet been found. It has yet to exist. For it is not the thinkable All, but the All given to us as a total reality, the All for which living fulfillment is to be achieved by our redemptive love, which comes from God. The rashness of human thought is opposed by the unattainable as the eternally indissoluble living shape. The shape is not thought, not evoked; it reveals itself.

And so, next to living revelation, all other religions sink back into religions of knowledge and the pagan-mythological religions, which knew living forms, are placed higher than the profoundly mystical and shapeless cognitive religions of the great Buddha. Form and life—these two burn in the heart of this redemption book, from which the mystic is spurned for elevating the I on its road to form.

All redemption is to become a formed whole. Our free deed of love, coming over the living, growing world of creation, forms pure, blind Being into a living superworld of the formed whole and matures growing life toward the Kingdom of God. The deed of love works, not like the artist, who only forms images of life, but as a living soul shaping real life toward its innermost meaning and thereby toward redemption. And the life of creation comes toward our love, turns toward redemption. The space and time of redemption are determined by that life, by the creation in which space and time are at home. Hence the moment is unequivocally, immovably established within the historical process. Each time has its special form of redemption. And the great historical forms of redemption demonstrate the position of the world clock. Thus, for us too, our era's great position of knowledge and experience must be traversed in a living way if we are to recognize—and profess—our present-day truth. It was only from that excess of enlivenment and affirmation of all life and personal destiny in all its heights and depths, it was only from that thoroughly alive relationship to reality, which only Goethe succeeded in achieving and which could only be attained at that moment—it was only from that superhuman isolation of later minds, that gigantic upward swelling toward individualism and relativism, that the tremendous will for truth could break forth, a will that can find repose again solely in God. It was only for us that the "*donec requiescat in te*" [until He comes to rest in you] could again become authentic life. Hence, pure faith is not enough—only he "who summons God with the two-fold prayer of the devout and the undevout will not be unheeded by Him."

It is clearly only in history, in which redemption takes place uniquely, that redemption becomes visible as the entrance of the eternal into time—which redemption transforms from the amorphous torrent of mere flow into a meaningful, eternity-touched shape of the hour. For the hour no longer belongs to the world of creation; "bells begin to strike the hour only in the kingdom of redemption." All redemption, as we know it from history, is a redemption from time to the shape of time; redemption to the hour and the day, the week and the year, in which life ripens toward the time of eternity, the Kingdom.

It is for the reasons just given that redemption presents itself in the cycle of the spiritual year, as it takes shape from the miracle of revelation. Judaism as the bearer of eternal life goes first. Within it, eternity has already returned to immediate life, caught in the seed of original existence. The Jew is born as a Jew. His birth makes him part of the holy nation and gives him a part in eternity, in redemption. For "there is only one community . . . that cannot pronounce the 'we' of its unity without hearing deep within the complementary 'are eternal'" [2:48]. All other nations are mortal in that they are tied to a specific land, a specific earthly home, for which the blood of their sons flows. "We alone trusted the blood and left the land . . . and were alone of all the nations on earth in redeeming our life from any fellowship with death" [2:48–49]. The land belongs "to the Jew in the deepest sense as only the land of his yearning, as—the Holy Land" [2:51]. The blood-fellowship alone makes the Jew a Jew, whereas every Christian, by reason of adhering to his earthly homeland, is pagan by birth, reaching Christianity only through an inner conversion, through the conversion in the sign of the cross. So Judaism has paganism outside of itself, the paganism that the Christian bears within himself and must overcome only throughout history, and can never fully overcome. That is why the Christian always lives in time and in the world, whereas the Jew is refused any participation in the temporal life of the surrounding world, for the sake of the eternal life that is his share. Land, language, custom, and law, in whose living development the Christian nations live, have, for the Jew, long since left the circle of the living. He has no part in those forms that shape Christianity into life: church and state. For, whereas the eternal lives in the Jew merely in his continual procreation, the Christian is always on the way. Christianity does not continue by means of procreation, but through its constant expansion in the sphere of historical life: through the mission.

Both Judaism and Christianity have drawn eternity down into time by the great division of all life according to its inherent eternal meaning: Judaism in the form of the pervasive immortality of its life; Christianity in the form of simultaneity, which is the principle of space and time and the fraternity that outsoars all human distinctions.

Neither Judaism nor Christianity has the entire truth, each has its share, and each thereby, in order to experience eternity, divides in its own way the even flow of time in the spiritual year. And thus the year itself becomes an image of the circle of redemption.

Separated, therefore, under various signs, in various circles of redemption, the Jew and the Christian, the bearers of the revelation, come before the face of God. Neither is whole unto itself. A final individual element remains in the relationship to the Eternal. No human structure, however ripe, is itself the truth. God alone is truth.

In this jubilant certainty, the book [*The Star of Redemption*] comes to an end: God is truth—not truth God, but God is truth. We—and here the subjectivity of individual standpoints is resolved—we are those who have eternally only a portion in truth. Not as the whole that it is and shall become, but only as a part allotted to us. And our task is to prove ourselves with this share: to say *verily* to truth.

In this way alone is death overcome: the cognitive viewpoint of the self, which has a knowledge that is individual, definite, and transitory, because it is always attached to a portion of individualized, doomed reality, claims, however, a share in the encroaching divine truth. Death is overcome when the eternal is professed and dying individuality is abandoned. Only the individual dies.

By stepping before the countenance of the divine truth that radiates everywhere, each of us in his place and in his time, speaking *verily* to our share in the truth, the share that the truth bestows, overcomes death and isolation in the fellowship of the living.

Truth lies not at the beginning, not in our having, but at the end, in our proving ourselves. The final thing demanded of us is trust, but trust is grand proclamation. "It is the very simplest thing in the world and for that very reason the most difficult thing" [3:210].

It is known to him who has written this book, which is so full of ardor and brightness, promise and eternity—but only for the man who trusts, the man who wants to believe and can believe. It is the enormous attempt at drawing faith, simple, immediate faith in God, into the life of cognition. There is no other way of saving our present point in time. Only faith can save us, the faith in the unity of truth, which all systems were incapable of proving, and which, in our time, was definitively, swept away by the tempest of life. But faith is not just demanded here, not just preached: faith is believed. The book is full of the light of revelation that it proclaims. At its peaks, the language itself becomes revelation. It finds words of love as no other book in our day; for here alone, as the path from God to man and from man through other men back to God, love has once again become the love that never ceases. All the eternal, age-old names regain their original life, become word and fire by the profession of those names.

And for this faith, this profession, the star of redemption finally flares up as the face of God itself. The eternal superworld of the formed whole sends to man as the last image the miracle of the countenance, not its own face, but the miracle of the divine countenance. For "truth cannot be uttered otherwise. It is only when we behold the star as the countenance that we have fully come beyond all possibility of possibilities and simply behold."

The image of Saïs is unveiled—but the dreadfully shattering image of the self, which is shown to the knower, becomes the unveiled countenance of God in the eternal superworld of the formed whole. And that removes from the unveiler the curse of the image of truth: He no longer sees himself in utter intensity and distortion as soon as he seeks truth in faith rather than knowledge. He beholds God.

It would be impossible and meaningless here to practice a "criticism" that does not spring from the inherent presumptions of this book, which has borrowed language from the elements of the world of old as well as the light of the superworld. As Rosenzweig says at one point, the concept of creation, with which he opens the innermost Being of the phenomenal world and its relationship to the divine and the human, cannot be taken as a scholarly or scientific hypothesis to be accepted or rejected according to proofs and counterproofs. Likewise, the entire rich, torrential, wide-branching book can only be accepted, beyond any demonstration, as a disclosure, illumination, and beholding of ultimate, eternal connections of Being. It may still seem too early to open our eyes to full truth after the immeasurable, dreadful separation from it; it may still be too early to behold God, who concealed Himself from us for so long in heavy fogs, clouds, and shrouds, in strident lightning and thunder; the entrance of theology into philosophy may at first remind us all too intimately of the support that the lame man offers the blind man; the bubbling fullness of life, which only just burst forth to us, may seem pressed and violated under an excess of construction, under the all-too-rigorous lines of truth and eternity—each of these protests is countered by this book with a radiant, overwhelming "*And yet.*" It means to make visible, to give shape to, what is as ineffable in its origin as in its end. The pathways of the radiant double triangle, which lead from the origin to the end, must cut sharp and solid through moving life, and must therefore, albeit living pathways, cut only life to shreds. And if we catch the utterance, that today only the devout man may philosophize, it strikes us, despite everything, as a veritable solution and redemption from the distress of this our age. For it is, after all, the living truth and not the thinking truth that Rosenzweig drives to a new revelation—and where would living truth ever be found for man if not in faith? Whatever one may feel about this book, written in the face of death and with its gaze upon God, it unveils in its depths the mortally wounded truth of our time, which nonetheless powerfully struggles for the truth's healing.

PART THREE

Epilogue

ABBREVIATIONS

BG&E	Nietzsche, Friedrich. *Beyond Good and Evil.*
Das Büchlein	*Das Büchlein vom gesunden und kranken Menschenverstand.* Edited by Nahum Glatzer. Düsseldorf: Joseph Melzer Verlag, 1964.
The Difference	Hegel, Georg Wilhelm Friedrich. *The Difference Between Fichte's and Schelling's System of Philosophy.* Translated by H. S. Harris and Walter Cerf. New York: State Univ. of New York Press, 1977.
"Ethics and Spirit"	Levinas, Emmanuel. "Ethics and Spirit." In *Difficult Freedom: Essays on Judaism.* Translated by Sean Hand. Baltimore: Johns Hopkins Univ. Press, 1990.
The Guide	Maimonides, Moses. *The Guide for the Perplexed.* Translated by Shlomo Pines. Chicago: Univ. of Chicago Press, 1963.
Twilight	Nietzsche, Friedrich. *Twilight of the Idols.*
Untimely Meditation	Nietzsche, Friedrich. *Untimely Meditations.* Translated by R. J. Hollingdale. Cambridge: Cambridge Univ. Press, 1983.
Das Wort	Ebner, Ferdinand. *Das Wort und die geistigen Realitäten.* Munich: Kösel Verlag, 1963.

References to Rosenzweig's texts are keyed to the following as they appear in Rosenzweig, Franz. *Der Mensch und sein Werk: Gesammelte Schriften,* vol. 3, *Zweistromland.* Edited by Reinhold and Annmarie Mayer. The Hague: Martinus Nijhoff, 1984.

References to *Der Stern der Erlösung* are to volume and page of the second edition: Berlin: Schocken Verlag, 1930: 1. *Anleitung zum jüdischen Denken;* 2. *Die Bauleute;* 3. *Bildung und kein Ende;* 4. *Hic et Ubique: Ein Wort an Leser und andre Leute;* 5. *Das Neue Denken;* 6. *Neues Lernen;* 7. *Der Stern der Erlösung;* 8. *"Urzelle" des Stern der Erlösung;* 9. *Das Wesen des Judentums;* 10. *Die Wissenschaft vom Menschen;* 11. *Zeit Ists.*

9

Retracing the Steps of Franz Rosenzweig

ALAN UDOFF

If one recalls the . . . system in its true
constitution, then one *longs* for a better,
more beautiful, more reassuring form.[1]
—F. W. J. von Schelling

This essay is intended as an introduction to the *new thinking* of
Franz Rosenzweig. It takes its bearings from Leo Strauss's eu-
logy:

Franz Rosenzweig is the founder of the Academy.

Franz Rosenzweig's idea was, in accordance with his avowed
purpose, politically intended. This man, who earned for himself such great rewards as a thinker and scholar in the service
of *Wissenschaft,* was not concerned with *Wissenschaft* as something "taken for granted," as something that did not require

legitimation before an other superior tribunal; he was concerned with Judaism. He maintained the vindication of our existence as Jews as the norm of any science of Judaism with a forcefulness that we are not able to forget. Franz Rosenzweig will always remain for all who strive after this science the admonisher of their proper duty.[2]

In speaking of "legitimation before an other superior tribunal," Strauss puts us in mind of Kant and the "call to reason to undertake *anew* the most difficult of all its tasks, namely, that of self-knowledge, and to institute a tribunal which will assure to reason its lawful claims."[3] From this tribunal, religion, its sanctity notwithstanding, cannot exempt itself.[4] It would undoubtedly be correct to understand Rosenzweig's vindication of Jewish existence with reference to these claims (2:702).[5] But, it must not be forgotten thereby that that vindication is intended as the measure of any "science of Judaism," and that in the end that science in its characteristically modern form depends upon a prior, ultimately prejudicial, rejection of revelation.[6] All of which is to say that as Strauss understood, it is with Spinoza—not the vindicator of Judaism, but "the greatest man of Jewish origin who had *openly* denied the truth of Judaism"[7]—rather than with Kant, that Rosenzweig is to be contrasted. This contrast is not the object of the present essay; it is concerned instead with the want, the lack, because of which research and learning, science and instruction are dying (3:494), the same want that Nietzsche saw in his own time: "culture can grow and flourish only out of life."[8] It is concerned, then, with death and life written in large letters.[9] In this respect, the place of Nietzsche may be indicated as follows: Nietzsche maintained the vindication of existence as the norm of any science with a forcefulness that Franz Rosenzweig was not able to forget.

For Rosenzweig, Nietzsche is the interval continuing in the philosophical period begun by Schopenhauer and whose end (7/1:13)—the *beyond* [*das Jenseits*] that philosophy as the identity of thinking and being cannot see (7/1:12)—is yet to come. In this period, Nietzsche stands as this new thing [*dies Neue*] "forcefully inserted into the riverbed of the development of conscious spirit from out of which it cannot be torn" (7/1:14). How is this "something new" [*etwas Neues*]—how is the substance of its instauration—to be understood? Nietzsche was the man who first knew and lived his life out of the unity of poet, saint, and thinker (7/1:14). He reoriginated philosophy in the ex-orbitancy of life beyond the closed circle of idealism's systematic representation. That originary life *as lived* annuls, at the same time that it preserves and elevates, the compass of that systematicity as it is set out in the triadic arcs of art, religion, and philosophy. In Nietzsche, life as transformation [*Verwandlung*] is *vindicated* before the tribunal of the absolute spirit. In Nietzsche, in the Nietzschean life, may be seen that *new* thing: life as *Aufhebung*. Nietzsche is the tribunal which those who must philosophize no longer can bypass [*vorbei* (7/1:15)].[10]

The account that Rosenzweig gives of Nietzsche is remarkable (7/1:14–15)[11] both for that which it omits and for that which it includes. What Nietzsche accomplished philosophically [*erphilosophiert*] under the headings Dionysiac, *Übermensch,* blond beast, and eternal return, Rosenzweig allows is today almost a matter of indifference. It is the exemplarity of the life that was of his own making, of one who "in the transformations of his conceptual images transformed himself," that endures. That transformation may be indicated in this way: Nietzsche is the end of that Augustinian beginning in which the question of self-knowledge found its rest in his recognition of having been made by God (the rest in which the theoreticality of *the question* itself [*ti esti*] finds repose) and the radical culmination of the project of self-making begun by Montaigne. With Nietzsche, the breath of the life of the living soul is breathed into the philosopher.

The perspectival point at back of Rosenzweig's portrayal of Nietzsche is the pedagogic *agon* of soul and *Geist*. The picture of Nietzsche the man reveals a soul without dread of height [*Höhe*], climbing after [*nachkletterte*] *Geist*—itself the daring climber [*Kletterer*]. Soul and *Geist* are thus kindred to each other by virtue of ascent.[12] In Nietzsche's words, they are the sisters in whose unity the futural elevation [*Höheit*] of the human is found.[13] This ascent extends even to the precipitous summit of madness, to the lawless limit of the furthermost [*wo es kein Weiter mehr gab*]: to the height that *as* height looks into the abyss, to the ripeness that holds falling within it.[14] It is the ascent in which the high and the low meet in Nietzsche's *own self* [*im eigenen Selbst*]. From this point onward, the image of the soul accompanied by *Geist* is ineffaceably established.

The great thinkers of the past, from the vantage of their own height, conceived the soul differently: as wet-nurse or schoolmistress to *Geist*. The memory of this tutorial relationship is embedded in *Geist* itself, which looks with dread at the four narrow [*eng*] walls in which it had grown large [*gross geworden*]—as if it were the swelling contents of a cup in want of overflowing.[15] We are not told how it comes about that *Geist* leaves the confinements of the soul's classroom (cf. 7/1:92–95), any more than we are at first told how it comes about that Zarathustra, at length tiring of his *Geist* and undergoing a change of heart, descends from his mountain heights to the lower world in order that he might become a man among men. But it is by right [*mit Recht*] that it is done (3:497): for this overflowing of the boundaries [*Grenze*] is life *as* lived [*ge-lebt* (3:493)]. Life entrusts itself [*vertrauen*] to a state of readiness [*Bereitschaft*]. Readiness is the ec-static, futural temporalization that is openness to the whole; it knows the whole in the actuality of that which is nearest, and in that way possesses the whole (3:500). Life confidently lived [*mit Vertrauen gelebt*], is one with the soul that shrinks before no height [*keine Höhe scheute* (7/1:15)] "with carefree step it goes over the threshold leading from today into tomorrow [*es geht mit sorglosem Fusse über die Schwelle, die aus dem Heute in Morgen führt*]" (3:500).

Life takes that street which, rounding itself into infinity, seems to the fearfully apprehensive [*dem Ängstlichen* (3:500)] to lose itself therein. Thus lived, it resists agonally (*wehrt sich*) the lifeless segmented claims [*Teilansprüche* (3:497)] that have not taken their place on the traversable yet endless circumference of the circle that is its *itinerarium* (3:500). These *Teilansprüche* live in the twilight of an appropriation [*Verwen-*

dung (7/1:17)] that, seeming whole, is yet no longer whole [*kein Ganzes mehr* (3:496; 4:509)]. They comprise—to employ a medical analogy in keeping with Rosenzweig's own affinity for such analogies—a lexicon of false positives, concepts (e.g., "personal life, personality, individuality") rendered useless through their philosophical appropriation (7/1:17). The variations in which they are proximally encountered (e.g., law, home, synagogue (3:495) exhibit a thematic sameness: each seeks for itself a safe and undisturbed little corner [*ein sicheres, ungestörtes Eckchen* (3:497)]). Each has lost its vital connection with the whole of life. Each, then, must be returned, thereby binding Jewish life into a unity [*das jüdische Leben zur Einheit* (3:496)]: law must again become commandment (2:707); learning again a *teaching* (2:701). The question of the *teachings* is paradigmatic.[16] The nineteenth century, which apportioned [*teilen*] everything into compartments (3:497), first brought to the teachings of Judaism, already "restricted [*eingeschränkt*] to the sumptuous poverty of a few fundamental concepts," "a practical and far-reaching earnestness" (2:702). What remains is "a dead booklearning called 'the science of Judaism'" (3:497). Rightly [*mit Recht*], in the presence of this death, life flows unconcernedly past [*das Leben flutet unbekümmert daran vorüber* (3:497)]. That right, the mark of which is its naturalness, appears then where our first or instinctual nature is still in place, foremost "to the instinct of youth, for youth still possesses that instinct of nature which remains intact until artificially and forcibly shattered by . . . education."[17] Accordingly, one day the pupil, having grown up, and enjoying his freedom and his unrestricted view of things [*unbegrenzte Aussicht*], goes *on his own way* [*ging seine eigenen Wege* (7/1:15)].

We are drawn, thereby, again to the tonic *eig-*.[18]

Rosenzweig's portrayal of Nietzsche culminates in that which Nietzsche exemplarily prepares and sets forth over against philosophy: "the human being in the utter singularity of his proper being [*Eigenwesen* (7/1:16)]." The path that leads to *das Eigentliche* had always been present in the actuality of the poets' and saints' existence, in the way in which their lives and their own souls [*eigene Seele*] were turned to the compass of the fatefulness of their calling. Nietzsche was that truly new being: the philosopher who, going undaunted on his way, incorporated in his own self [*im eigenen Selbst*] the wholeness in whose unity to the last the boundary between high and low, soul and Geist, man and thinker, no longer existed (7/1:15). There is a common ground underlying these *passages*—the text and that to which it looks. The turn [*Wendung*] to that ground is made difficult by the loss—through appropriation [*Verwendung*]—of the language in which its topography had traditionally, and thus recognizably, been written. The way for those who would undertake this turn is through a new learning, one that leads, out of the confidence that is at its heart, from the periphery back to the center (6:507–8)—the ownness that *chordally* invokes the ownmost: *Wie spricht ein Geist zum andern Geist.*[19]

The metaphor, to be sure, may mislead. Time, the secret of the *new teaching* (5:149), is in its way consecutive. The verticality of what is harmonically sounded too readily corresponds to the height of the symbol and the breadth of the eternal.[20] It is necessary, then, to listen to that which is invoked, to the intervals of its resonance, in several ways.[21] The topos that Rosenzweig denominates *das Eigentliche,* to which he repeatedly turns in his Nietzsche portrait, is key to the text. The *Eigentliche* is a measure of the distance that separates the defining concreteness of the new thinking from the abstractness or ideality of the old: "Certainly, the word of the . . . philosophers originates in the personal life. However, it is precisely in becoming the . . . philosophical word that it cuts itself off from this, and for that reason never speaks to the 'concrete' personality in man, but only to the 'ideal.'"[22] Ebner identifies, here, the moment of turning-from that sets the stage for the appearance of philosophy in the role of totalizing or identificatory reason. This configuration of philosophy is at the endpoint of the Cartesian construction, and at the origins of postmodern thought. It completes the Cartesian doubt in deconstructing the reconciliation of self, thought, and world through asserting the recalcitrant, unpossessable *Eigentlichkeit* of that which is by virtue of being other.[23] Rosenzweig's assessment of the philosophical tradition from Ionia to Jena (7/1:17–18) is kindred to the origins, if not to the ends, of this thought. The pupil who, having grown up, sets out upon his own way [*seine eigenen Wege*], is thus beyond ideality—that is to say, he now knows the ownmost possibility of existence.[24] He knows that he will die. It is not this death, however, but the specter of lifelessness from which it has at last unfettered itself, that, at this place, fills the pupil's thoughts. He thinks only with horror of the four narrow walls of the soul's classroom in which he had grown up—the soul-like [*seelenhaft*] torpor in which *Ungeist* had endured the imprisonment of the soul [*die Haft der Seele*]: "Thus, precisely, *Geist* enjoyed its being free of the soul-like torpor in which *Ungeist* passed its days" (7/1:15). How may this be understood?

Imprisonment is the condition of *Ungeist;* freedom is the essence of *Geist*.[25] Where that freedom manifests itself in man essentially—and where the essence of man is essentially revealed—is in his own deed.[26] The deed bears, thereby, beyond the order of contingency wherein it displays itself, that which is essential. It is in the ownness [*das Eigene*] of the deed that that which is actualized [*das Eigentliche*] in the essential takes place. That actuality is the subject [*das eigentliche Ich* (7/2:112)] revealed in the deed that is its own, and through the summons of the *you* that calls it forth (10:646). The originary constitution of calling-forth as address—as the calling-of the other—discloses the topography of the ground from out-of-which calling evokes response; for that which in the foreground is figurally present in hiding is not the *idea* of one who hides, but that very one—"man hides himself"—who stands upon a ground from whose configuration he is called-forth: yet "he does not answer, he remains speechless" (7/2:113).

The silence of concealment, in the forms of both address and response, dwells in the place of the indefinite [*das Unbestimmte*] and merely indicative [*das Blos hinweisende* (7/2:113)].[27] The silence of the indefiniteness of the "you" of the divine address thus demarcates a region of being: the going-out-from

[*Ausweg*], on which ground silence appears as "the human being hypostatizes [*vergegenständlicht sich selbst*] itself into 'man'"
(7/2:113). The indefiniteness of the divine "Where are you?"
belongs then to *creation,* which includes not only beings but
that in which they take place. The "Where are you?" creates
that into which man may go-out-from. It creates not a man
who, out of fear of discovery, hides, but hiding itself.[28] From
that into which man has gone-out, he must be summoned
back for the *entering-into* [*eintreten*] that is his end. Man must
be cut off from the retreat [*Ausweg*] of general concepts; that
which cannot flee—the utterly particular that is beyond conceptuality—must be revealed.[29] Thus, the vocative call-to [*Anruf*] steps into the place of the indefinite [*an Stelle des
unbestimmten . . . tritt der Vokativ, der Anruf*], and calls man forth
out of the proper name [*Eigenname*] that God created for him
(7/2:113). In *revelation* the seed of *redemption* is already present.
That is, the *calling-to* that addresses freedom out-of distance,
and thus names the *there,* speaks in the vocative of summons
to the *there* in the distance of the evocation or calling-forth
where man waits.[30] Calling-forth, exemplarily entering into
the distance, summons the one who is free for the sake of going-in to what is real—into life. In that going-in, the *there* in
which man hides on the way out from life [*Ausweg*] becomes
the entrance or initiation into [*Eingang*] the *here:* the place
where, in the keeping of the confidence that is trust, "pure
readiness" declares: "Here am I" (7/2:113).

These topoi are representative of the eidetic structure of
Rosenzweig's *maître récit.*[31] Thus, the story of the call-to philosophical[32] man is complementary to the story of the call-to

man.[33] The philosopher "distrustfully [*misstrauisch*] withdraws into the protected spellbinding circle [*Zauberkreis*] of his wonder," where he is safe [*sicher*] in its dumbfoundedness [*Starrheit*]—repeating, thereby, the condition of the man who, called-to, and seeking safety, fled into the refuge of generality's call-to the *you,* where he remains dumb [*stumm*] and obdurate [*verstockt*].[34] Similarly, the imagined philosopher's place within a *Zauberkreis* extends to the configuration of his alter ego who, for that reason, is not simply to be conjured by a spell [*Zauber*] to entreat his response—but by a more powerful spell [*stärkere Zauber* (7/2:113)] to break the mirror that holds him in the thrall[35] of *Geist* returning to itself—in which the I discovers itself [*Sich selber entdeckt es—nicht etwa das Du* [(7/2:113)]: the mirror that holds him in the thrall of *Geist's* return.[36]

That which presents itself here—the reflection of philosophy—is the last thing before the distance awaiting *Eingang*: "The essence of philosophy, on the contrary, is a bottomless abyss for personal idiosyncrasy [*Eigentümlichkeiten*]. . . . For reason, finding consciousness caught in particularities, only becomes philosophical speculation by raising itself to itself, putting its trust only in itself [*sich anvertraut*] and the Absolute which, at that moment becomes its object."[37]

In place of that essence, that is, in-place-of the science of logic [*Wissenschaft der Logik*], stands the logic that is not timeless [*nicht zeitlos*]: it is the logic of the real [*Sie ist die Logik des wirklichen*]. Into the chain of the temporality of its calling and tradition one enters (*eintreten*) only in this way: Here there is no question of mistrust. Here you live by trust.[38]

❦

Freedom is the *Eingang* into life that *as* entrance crosses the threshold of that which had confined it. That which lies behind the threshold is not always recognized for what it is. The narrowness of its enclosure appears as such from the other that stands over against it. This narrowness has no properly ontic measure. What defines or delimits it is the distantiation that constitutes its relationship to the other that is beyond:

> Whoever you might be: in the evening step out
> from your room, therein you know all;
> as the last thing before the distance lies your house:
> whoever you might be.[39]

No measure is to be found here in the difference or distance between room and house; nor is the entrance that constitutes taking leave of them a deduction from any calculation of *Ferne.* The going-in that has as its object the knowable world is not essentially different from the room that Rilke describes. To see it for what it is, then, requires that one look at it out of the wholeness of the humanly lived life:[40] "The age asks nothing less of man today than this: Who are you? Who do you wish to be? It is to you as whole man, not to a part [*Teil*] of your being, that the question is addressed."[41] The question summons man to step into the going-in [*Eingang*]. The primordiality of questioning, here signified by the familiar *du*— the address in which the space of touching is implicitly opened, is directed toward *some* listener: *wer.* Audition replaces sight. The primacy of life replaces the primacy of the theoretical life. The wholeness of a human existence replaces intellectual virtue."[42]

Entrance into this wholeness manifests itself in the other, ex-orbitant to philosophy's imitation of the end of its desire: "Until now, all philosophical interest had revolved around the knowable *All;* even man had been allowed as an object of philosophy only in his relation to this *All*" (7/1:14).

The motion of this revolution is epicyclical. A periodic retrogression prefaces the permissible appearance of the human, existing only in relation [*Verhältnis*] to the appropriative *All*.[43]

The holding [*halten*] of the human takes place in the *Begriff* [*greifen*/grasp] of *Wesen:* "'Essence' is the concept under which [i.e., the height from which] the world of objects . . . arranges itself—essence, the universal, that gathers all particularity into itself, because it 'precedes' all particularity" (8:132).

The arrangement of the world of objects under essence assimilates difference to kindredness, irrespective of—that is, without looking to—the orders of being: "Because it knows men overall, 'all' men, or the world overall, all things, are brother to each other; *for this reason* the Stoic 'loves,' the Spinozist 'loves' his neighbor" (8:132).

The measure of existence in the distantiation of its wholeness is configured in the other at this point—and tangent to the orbit of the knowable *All* [*den Kreis des wissbaren All* (7/1:16)]:

> Against [*Gegen*] such love that originates out of the essence, the universal, stands [*steht*] the other [love] [*die andre*] that ascends out of the event [*Geschehnis*], that is, out of the most particular that there is. (8:132)

Now an other [*ein andres*], the living man, independently [*selbstständig*] stepped forward [*trat*] over against [*gegenüber*] the knowable world, a derisive one[44] in the face of the all, opposing to every allness [*Allheit*] and universality the "unique and his own." (7/1:14)

In stepping forward, that which was *Gegenstand* becomes the form of the other that stands by itself [*selbstständig*] over against [*gegenüber*]. In stepping forward, the out-of-which is given along with it, and, therewith, what is not yet given in the *Gegen:* the originary place of the measure: "The concept of order of this world is thus not the universal, neither the arche nor the telos, neither the natural nor the historical unity, but rather the particular, the event [*Ereignis*], *not beginning or end, but center of the world*" (8:133). Thus stepping forward is the mark of the living, *geistlich,* one.[45]

The *narrowness* of the four imprisoning walls may be taken now as indexical. A lifelessness, that is, a withdrawal from the concrete, from *das Eigentlich,* is at work in its design—in the same way that it was seen to be at work in the fate of the teachings. In passing structurally to Rosenzweig's description of the narrowing [*einschränken*] of the (Jewish) *teachings,* that is, their reduction to the poverty of a few fundamental concepts [*der Armut einiger Grundbegriffe* (2:702)], a synonymy is established between the lifeless and the poor. Whatever figure comes in that guise may appropriate *Geist,* but it can neither know nor teach it truly; dwelling in the heights that are the turning-from life, it knows *Geist* by virtue of height as such and the kindredness of all such turning [*hē tēs psuchēs periagogē*]. But it cannot know or grasp [*fassen* (7/1:16)] that which can only be lived, that is, the striving for that height that belongs to *Geist* and, after Nietzsche, that belongs in common to soul. Here, those who come in this guise are the philosophers for whom philosophy is the cool height [*kühle Höhe*] to which they had slipped away from the mists [*Dünsten*] of the plains where the breath of life that was the soul was breathed into *a* man.[46] It is Nietzsche who plays for Rosenzweig the animating force in the story of the creation of *a* philosophical man. Philosophy is the dichotomy of thought, the knowable whole [*das wissbare All*] and allness and generality [*Allheit und Allegemeinheit*], on the one hand, and man, the living man [*der lebendige Mensch*], and the unique one and his unpossessable particularity [*der "Einzige und sein Eigentum"*], on the other (7/1:14). In locating philosophy's boundary in the one that *lives,* in the life that *as* lived is beyond boundary, the guise in which philosophy comes may now be seen properly as a form of death, the poverty [*Armut*] that has as its end the reduction of the manifold [*Vielheit* (7/1:18)] to a few fundamental concepts—the whole on the basis of relationship to which man is allowed as an *object* [*Gegenstand*] of philosophy (7/1:14). Philosophy comes in the guise of that which impoverishes the *Geist* of man, that which is the death of the living man—over against which that *Armut im Geiste* in which his salvation lies calls.[47] In Nietzsche's own self, dichotomy—and therewith the old thinking—is overcome. A unity to the last, he is thus present in the beginning (7/1:15). At this beginning, so its story tells, there is temptation as well.

In Rosenzweig's version of the story (7/1:15–16) philosophy promises to give the one wholly specific man—the living man—who had thus become a power [*Macht*] over his philosophy, *Geist,* in exchange for selling [*verkauften*] his soul. He repeats thereby Goethe's version of this story, where Faust, in the confines of his accumulated books [*Beschränkt mit diesem Bücherhauf* (ln. 402)], addresses the tempter of his soul: "What would you, poor Devil, offer?/ Was a man's *Geist* in its high striving ever grasped by your like?" (ln. 1675–6) It is in this guise, in this likeness, that philosophical temptation comes. But, now, to no avail; for the philosophizing man—not the one transformed into or cashed in for some spiritual or intellectual thing [*nicht der ins Geistige umgesetzte*], but philosophizing man, endowed with a soul [*beseelte*], who had achieved mastery [*mächtig geworden*] over philosophy—that man, from the start beyond the grasp of philosophical knowing [*wissen*], and now to be recognized [*anerkennen*] as such, as ungraspable [*nicht begreifen*], sees the offer of this appropriated *Geist* as the frozen breath of his living soul: the death mask of an intention.[48] It is this mask that must be removed if, in man's entry into the innermost sanctuary of the divine truth, he is to see that countenance that is *like his own* [*ein Antlitz gleich dem eigenen* (7/3:210)]. The gates to this sanctuary—unlocked by God [*Gott . . . schloss mir die Pforten des Heiligtums auf*]—are the gates into the quotidian in which life lives, and where one may be shown that which lives beyond life [*ein Leben jenseits des Lebens*]. That which is seen in this *beyond* [*das Jenseits*] has already been perceived in the midst [*Mitte*] of life, where it is ever in danger of succumbing to philosophy and to the confinements of its appropriative understanding of *das Eigentlich* [*beschränkt auf das Eigentliche*][49]—for the gates are sealed with many seals in the keeping of the Old Thinking. Thinking, which in the truth of its nature can have no tradition, has become a history, behind the gates of whose cave the modern experiences its determining instructions ready-made.[50] It is Nietzsche who unlocks for thinking [*Denken*] that new land [*Neuland* (7/1:17)], so that besouled *Geist* may pass through the gates that lead beyond the knowable world, the circumference of whose being is one with the thought that thinks it, into life.

In the *calling-to* and *-forth* for the sake of entering into life, there is distance: for after that which is the last thing before the distance lies the *going-in* of life. Life is that which is nearest the distance. That is to say: it is not that which is nearest simply. Trust, as that out of which life is entered-in, knows only this nearest [*Vertrauen weiss nur vom Nächsten* (3:500)]. It must know, then, as well, the distance: for the pure readiness into which it passes—the utter disposability of having become wholly ear (7/2:114)[51] and having yet not received commandment—remains thereby a *leading-in* [*Einleitung*]. Until the distance that separates hearing and commandment has been crossed, the measure of readiness is still taken by the *there* of its *calling-forth*: in the emptiness of its being ready to receive, its measure is the content that it is now *without* [*ohne Inhalt* (7/2:113)]; the essence that it is now *without* [*ohne Wesen* (7/2:113)]. *Das Ohne* is the measure of this distance.[52]

This structure is evident in the way in which Rosenzweig sees the renewal of Jewish being: it is *called-to* in its peripheral existence; it is *called-forth* from the *habitus* of its alienation—its customary forms of self-understanding (e.g., "pointing out 'relations' between the Jewish and non-Jewish," or "apologetics"); it must do *without* these forms, in order to "find a place to turn in [*Einkehr*] in the heart of our life"; "and it must have confidence [*Vertrauen*] that this heart is a Jewish heart" (6:508). It is not only the forms of essential definition that must be given up—but the form of the essential: The "*dwelling and living* in the heart of Judaism" that is still far in the distance [*noch weit davon entfernt*] is a consequence of the need for education through points of view [*gesichtspunkte* (9:526)]. The Jewish people, en masse, must still believe in "essence" because it does not yet *essent* (or: "pressence") [*Sie muss noch an "Wesen" glauben, weil sie noch nicht west* (9:526)].[53] Although these standpoints are yet necessary, "the goal of this education lies *beyond* [*jenseits*]"—as does the goal of Judaism: "The goal is not 'essence' *of* Judaism, but the whole Judaism, not essence at all, but life" (9:526).

The inner accord of education and life recalls the image of Rosenzweig eulogized by Strauss, and along with it the image of Nietzsche. That recollection is securely fixed in the resemblances borne by certain passages in *On the Uses and Disadvantages of History for Life* and certain passages of Rosenzweig's. The texts in question occupy a foreground that is still determined by the perspective at back of Rosenzweig's portrayal of Nietzsche: the pedagogic *agon* in which *Geist,* freed from the narrow confinements of its tutelage, may seek its education out of life. The condition of that confinement as presented by Nietzsche embraces,[54] as it does for Rosenzweig, the totality of culture—the traditions that inform it, and the institutions and assemblages that embody it:

culture (*Kultur*) can grow and flourish only out of life. . . . The education of German youth, however, proceeds from precisely this false and unfruitful conception of culture: its goal, viewed in its essence, is not at all the free cultivated man but the scholar, the man of science, . . . who stands aside from life so as to know it unobstructedly; its result, observed empirically, is the historical-aesthetic cultural philistine, the precocious and up-to-the-minute babbler about state, church, and art, the man who appreciates everything, the insatiable stomach which nonetheless does not know what honest hunger and thirst are. (117)

we are without culture [*Bildung*], more, we are ruined for living, for right and simple seeing and hearing, for happily seizing what is nearest [*das Nächste*] and most natural to us, and do not possess even the basis of a culture, because we are not even convinced we have genuine life in us. Fragmented and in pieces, dissociated almost mechanically into an inner or an outer, . . . mistrusting any feeling of our own [*ohne Vertrauen zu jeder eignen Empfindung*] . . . perhaps I still have the right to say of myself *cogito, ergo sum,* but not *vivo, ergo cogito.*[55] Empty 'being' is granted me, but not full and green 'life': the feeling that tells me I exist warrants to me only that I am a thinking creature, not that I am a living one . . . . Only give me life, then I will create a culture for you out of it!—Thus cries each individual of this generation and all those individuals will recognize one another from this cry. Who is to give them this life? (119–20)

The Academy for the Science of Judaism, of which Rosenzweig was the founder, had this as its end: "The teacher will awaken [*bringen*] through and through in the existence of the community a new liveliness" (11:478). This awakening bears, then, the marks of life itself—which become legible in that to which it has given birth:

> Instead of placing before those who draw near thirsting for knowledge a whole systematically worked out in terms of its content [*inhaltlich*], so that they may pass through it step by step—just as a university student is faced with the edifice of a science complete in outline and pending in particulars, something that he himself is not, but something in which he will and should make himself at home—instead of placing before one such a whole, it should content itself with making a mere beginning, to begin at the merely opportune moment. And it would begin with its own mere beginning: with speaking-space [*Sprechraum*] and speaking-time [*Sprechzeit*]. (3:501)

The one who begins thus is in need of nothing else than readiness:

> Whoever would help him, can give him nothing other than the empty forms of being ready which he by himself and only by himself may fill. Whoever gives him more gives him less. Only the empty forms, in which something may happen, are allowed to be held in readiness,[56] only—'Space and Time.' Really nothing other than this: a speaking-space and a speaking-time. (3:500)

The a priori forms of sensibility are brought hereby within the parameters of *Sprachdenken*. The transcendental ideality of their limit is replaced in the actualizing forms of speech that know God, world, and man. It is into the e-vocative openness of this speaking, and that onto which it opens, that the

Jewish individual is called-forth from the alienation of the periphery back to the center—*von der Peripherie ins Zentrum*. Both Jewish learning and Jewish life are thus called-to (6:507–8). Here, written in these large letters, the forces and forms of death and life in the *progressus* of *Geist* may be read.[57] There remains, however, a subtext that no reading may thoughtfully neglect. The metaphor in which the concerns of this essay have come to converge—what one may speak of as the master metaphor in Rosenzweig's representation of Jewish alienation and its overcoming: the relationship of periphery and center—originates in Schelling's discussion of the relationship of freedom and evil.[58] A very different topological reading would follow from thinking through this origination. It, too, would take its bearings from Leo Strauss's recollection of Franz Rosenzweig, but this time from Strauss's recollection of him as one "whose name will always be remembered when informed people speak about existentialism."[59]

Notes

Index

Notes

1. Introduction

1. Two reviews of the 1921 edition of the *Star* won Rosenzweig's approval, the one by Margarete Susman wholly, and the one by Hans Ehrenberg with one reservation (see 40–41). These reviews are included in the present volume, 105–11 and 112–20, respectively.

2. Rosenzweig had already prepared "The New Thinking" by the beginning of 1925. At that time he sent the manuscript to Martin Buber, asking him if he thought it was "publishable" [Druckenswert] (*Franz Rosenzweig: Der Mensch und sein Werk: Gesammelte Schriften,* vol. 1, *Briefe und Tagebücher, 2. Band: 1918–1929* [The Hague: Martinus Nijhoff, 1979], 1024. Hereafter referred to as *B & T*). Much later, in a letter dated 28 December 1936, Buber wrote, with full approval: "The essay 'The New Thinking,' by my deceased friend, Franz Rosenzweig, which you will find in his book, *Land of Two Rivers* [*Zweistromland: Kleinere Schriften zur Religion und Philosophie* (Berlin, 1926, 240ff.)], places *I and Thou* in the context of related thought" (*The Letters of Martin Buber: A Life of Dialogue,* ed. Nahum N. Glatzer and Paul Mendes-Flohr [New York: Schocken, 1991], 454). References to "The New Thinking" are given below as (*NT,* XX); the pagination is keyed to the essay as it appears in the present volume.

3. For a description of the Patmos Circle and the related publi-

cation *Die Kreatur,* see Harold Stahmer's *"Speak That I May See Thee!" The Religious Significance of Language* (New York: Macmillan, 1968), 121–24. The Patmos Circle (1915–1923) challenged the credibility of teaching history, society, and language in monologues. The original members included Eugen Rosenstock-Huessy, Leo Weismantel, Werner Picht, Hans Ehrenberg, and Karl Barth. The editors of *Die Kreatur* (1926–1930), Joseph Wittig, Martin Buber, and Victor von Weizsäcker, as well as the contributors—who included Rosenzweig, his cousins Hans and Rudolf Ehrenberg, Karl Barth, Leo Weismantel, Werner Picht and Nicholas Berdyaev—shared the same concerns. Rosenzweig wrote of these men with whom he was in conversation: "The dialogue that these monologues make between one another I consider the whole truth" (Stahmer, 123). Rosenstock-Huessy, who personally introduced (or, more accurately, drove) Rosenzweig to the speech-thinking method of philosophy and life, and who was largely responsible for Rosenzweig's turn to belief in God, expressed the purpose of the editors of *Die Kreatur:* "*The Creature* represented the sum of the struggles of Kierkegaard, Feuerbach, Dostoevsky, Nietzsche and William James. They had all discovered that no one has really anything to say, if they all say the same thing. The creature does not speak as God does. A husband does not speak as his wife, nor does a Christian as a Jew, nor a child as a professor. For that very reason and solely for that reason are they able to speak to, and must they speak to, one another. . . . What the editors of *The Creature* discovered, were the spiritually nourishing processes experienced by genuinely speaking and existentially thinking persons" (Stahmer, 122).

4. Nahum N. Glatzer, *Franz Rosenzweig: His Life and Thought* (New York: Schocken, 1953), 145.

5. By 1924 Rosenzweig had been the head of the Freies Jüdisches Lehrhaus for three years. The confusion and assumption among these readers may well have stemmed from their association

of Rosenzweig with the Lehrhaus. Under Rosenzweig's auspices, one of the main aims of this school was, indeed, to bring about a return to a living Judaism, primarily through the study of biblical and classical texts. See his various writings on the subject: in the section "Zum jüdischen Lernen," in *Zweistromland*, Nijhoff edition, 1984, pp. 459–517; in the little volume *On Jewish Learning*, ed. Nahum N. Glatzer (New York: Schocken, 1955); and in the section "Renaissance of Jewish Learning and Living" in *Franz Rosenzweig: His Life and Thought*, ed. Nahum N. Glatzer (New York: Schocken, 1953), 214–50.

6. See Gershom Scholem's review of the *Star*, "Franz Rosenzweig and His Book, *The Star of Redemption*," in *The Philosophy of Franz Rosenzweig*, ed. Paul Mendes-Flohr (Hanover, N.H.: Univ. Press of New England, 1988), 20–41.

7. In the *Star*, Rosenzweig shows admiration for the first bravely speaking individuals who, not as poets, not as statesmen, but as philosophers, put their own full-bodied, self-consciously experiential persons into their writing. See pages 7–9 in the *Star*, for how Rosenzweig reacts favorably to Kierkegaard, Schopenhauer, and Nietzsche.

8. Rosenzweig is emphatic with regard to any attempt at imagining limitations in God's powers to relate to the creature, as well as with regard to the folly of fancying that one can manipulate God. In "The New Thinking" Rosenzweig is careful to explain this. Whereas the "old thinking" limits itself to questions of essence, the "new thinking" asks questions of relationship. This, of course, does not mean that during the span of time in which the "old thinking" thrived, from the days of Greek antiquity until Hegel and Hegelianism, authentic relationships between God and the human being could not take place. Nor does it mean that only the Jew and Christian had such relationships. God, according to Rosenzweig, did not create religion, but the world. Rosenzweig's careful, emphatic explanation of all this reads:

The temples of the gods have rightly fallen, their statues rightly stand in the museum, their worship, as far as it was set in order and codified, may have been a single enormous error—but the invocation that called out to them from a tormented breast, and the tears shed by the Carthaginian father, who offered up his son as a sacrifice to Moloch, cannot have remained unheard, nor unseen. Or is God supposed to have waited for Sinai or even for Golgotha? No, as little as there are roads leading from Sinai or from Golgotha by which he may be reached with certainty, so little could he have refused to meet even the one who sought him on the mountain trails surrounding Olympus. There is no temple built which would be so near to him that would permit man to be confident of this nearness, and none which would be so far from him that his arm could not easily reach even to there, no direction out of which he could not come, no block of wood in which he does not at some time take up a dwelling, and no Psalm of David which always reaches his ear. (*NT,* 91)

9. Rosenzweig's designation of his philosophical method as "Sprachdenken" [speech-thinking] and the notion of the "speech-thinker" or "speaking-thinker" will be dealt with below.

10. Rosenzweig likes Hamann, and writes of him in 1925, the same year he was writing "The New Thinking": "Denn Poesie ist zwar die Muttersprache des menschlichen Geschlechts—wir brauchen die Hamann-Herdersche Weisheit nicht zu verleugnen." That is: "Poetry is indeed the mother tongue of the human being—we must not deny the wisdom of Hamann and Herder." ("Die Schrift und das Wort" [Scripture and word] in *Zweistromland,* Nijhoff edition, 1984, 782).

11. Rosenzweig, in his introduction to Hermann Cohen's Jewish writings, describes the rare and momentous event in a nation's

history when a great poet and a great philosopher meet in a national spirit. In the case of Germany the great poet was Goethe and the great philosopher was Kant. The quote is long, to give the full sense of how Rosenzweig perceived that literally there was something new in the air in which a new kind of thinking was meant to breathe—and was overdue—and could breathe only by virtue of the unique German air:

> The German university, as it existed until the outbreak of the War, owes its meaning, for which there is no comparison in the other countries of our cultural circle, to a unique coincidence of national and world historical developments. It is a wholly recent formation. Berlin, the new establishment of 1811, puts up the new type for the first time institutionally, after Jena had made it fully visible in the last decade of the last century in magnificent, but quickly wilted, blossoming. Early stages can be followed mostly in Göttingen up to the middle of the century, in Halle till beyond the middle of it. But since the beginning of the new century, precisely out of Jena and connected with a diaspora of its professors, there starts a spreading of the new spirit, the spirit from Jena, first to the newly established or rediscovered universities of the south, which then from the establishment of Berlin into the two next decades, seizes all German universities and determines permanently their spiritual physiognomy.
>
> What then is this new thing whereby the German professor of the nineteenth century, for his own consciousness as well as in the eyes of his fellow-citizens, became something which neither his predecessor in the eighteenth century nor his colleague outside of the German cultural region was: the appointed and responsible guardian over the soul of the nation, the "philosopher-king" as it were of the Platonic politics? How

did the teacher of a youth which prepares itself for office and earning and in addition has its fling if possible—for this remains also here as anywhere and now like in olden days the plain everyday of this profession—how did he come to such a festively heightened self-assurance, which, by the fact that the nation acknowledged it, became a life-forming reality? A condition which still around 1900 was so specifically German that a German professor who travelled to America at that time was forced to explain to the people that they should not look at him as a schoolmaster for nineteen-year-old boys, but rather as—precisely as a German professor.

The answer is already indicated by the decisive position of Jena in the historical process sketched above. In the Jena of this decade that unique coincidence occurred, that a great moment of thought, always world historical according to its nature, harmonized in an harmonious striking of the hour with a great moment of language, always national-historical according to its nature. If Plato had to banish the great art of his people from his Ideal State, if the thinking of the Middle Ages and even still of the Renaissance took place in the hereafter of a world language beyond the living national languages, if just before this great moment Kant could write his *Aesthetics* without really knowing anything of Goethe, and Goethe just at that time, that is, not until after Italy, took the first cool notice of the *Critique of Reason,* which had appeared a good decade previously, so there now happened—first in Goethe's and Schiller's coming together, then in the confession of Fichte and Schelling to Goethe, accompanied by Friedrich Schlegel's trumpet sounds, lastly in the confessions to the two great poets by Hegel, finalizing as ever—so there now happened the world-historical miracle: the universal philosophy celebrated its reconciliation with the national culture, the language of poets gave form to the thoughts of the thinkers. In this way there arose what is called German Idealism, Germany's rightful title to the spiritual [*geistig*] supremacy which actually it had practised throughout the nineteenth century. Kant could not have exercised this power, as little as the aloneness of their appearance made a still more powerful impression on the mind than any of the later forms. Only the confluence of the two streams, which came from these two men, has established that world power of the German spirit [*Geist*].

From: "Einleitung in die Akademieausgabe der jüdischen Schriften Hermann Cohens," in *Zweistromland: Kleinere Schriften zu Glauben und Denken,* ed. Reinhold and Annemarie Mayer (The Hague: Martinus Nijhoff, 1984), pp. 177–79. Rosenzweig wrote this Introduction in the fall of 1923, and it was originally published with the posthumous three-volume collection of Hermann Cohen's Jewish writings [*Hermann Cohens Jüdische Schriften,* ed. Bruno Strauss (Berlin: C. A. Schwetschke & Sohn Verlag, 1924)]. It can also be found in the 1926 edition of *Zweistromland,* and in the *Kleinere Schriften* of 1937.

12. On 21 April 1927, Rosenzweig wrote to Jacob Rosenheim (1870–1965), the founder of Agudat Israel, an Orthodox anti-Zionist party, in the form of an essay, entitled "Die Einheit der Bibel: Eine Auseinandersetzung mit Orthodoxie und Liberalismus" [The unity of the Bible: An argument between orthodoxy and liberalism] (*Zweistromland,* pp. 831–35). Both points of view insist on the unity of the Bible, but Orthodoxy discredits science. In supplementary remarks appended to the letter-essay, Rosenzweig contends: "If science and religion attempt to ignore each other while yet having knowledge of each other, then both are on shaky ground. There is only one truth. No honest man can pray to a God whose existence he denies as a scientist. And whoever prays cannot at the same time

deny God. This does not mean that the scientist is to discover God in his test tube or historical document. But it does mean that the content of test tube or historical document does not exist without God. The object of science is not God but the world. But God has created the world, and thus the object of science." (Translated in Nahum Glatzer, *Franz Rosenzweig: His Life and Thought,* 209–10.)

13. For a lengthy treatment of the question of faith and reason, see Rosenzweig's lecture notes for six classes on the subject, "Glauben und Wissen," in *Zweistromland,* 581–95.

14. In *Letters of Martin Buber,* 345. Hans Trüb (1889–1949) was a psychiatrist in Zurich, and a friend of Buber's.

15. Nahum N. Glatzer, "The Frankfort Lehrhaus" in the *Leo Baeck Institute Year Book,* vol. 1 (London: East and West Library, 1956), 109–10.

16. In the review by Scholem of 1921 mentioned above, which he reaffirmed unaltered in 1930 (reprinted in *The Philosophy of Franz Rosenzweig,* ed. Paul Mendes-Flohr), Scholem discusses the mystical aspects, but by 1974 he had honed his critique regarding the detection of mystical concepts in several Jewish thinkers' writings. He observes the following: "Above all, however, concepts were introduced which in a disguised form—and denying their origin—adopted mystical concepts. That is true of authors as different as Kaufmann Kohler, Hermann Cohen, Franz Rosenzweig, and Martin Buber. They all polemicized against mysticism while borrowing its metaphors in case of need. . . . Rosenzweig's and Buber's disquisitions on this point, though executed within the framework of a philosophy of the dialogue between man and God, fundamentally acknowledge only one kind of Revelation—the mystical one, even though they refuse to call it by that name." (See Gershom Scholem, "Reflections on Jewish Theology," in *On Jews and Judaism in Crisis: Selected Essays* [New York: Schocken, 1976], 272–73.)

17. One early reviewer of the *Star,* a Prof. Dr. S. Frank, also con-

sidered Rosenzweig to be a mystic. He has a review that appeared in *Philosophische Monatshefte der Kant-Studien,* vol. 332/1/2, (1923?) Berlin.

> A strange, philosophically highly significant, book at the same time fitting in none of the conventional forms of philosophical research. It is a mystical philosophy (or theology), which consciously distances itself from the methods of pure philosophical thinking. . . . In opposition to philosophy the author wants to base his research on religious belief, on mystical experience. At the same time, however—and this is the paradox in the form of his research—he offers a wholly remarkable system, carefully thought through with the highest logically analytical energy, externally unbrokenly perfect, metaphysical. There is scarcely in the whole of world literature of mysticism a work which would be as systematic as that of Rosenzweig.

18. There are many examples of Rosenzweig's "healthiness," both from his own pen and from other's accounts, from 1922 to 1929, when he lived with amyotrophic lateral sclerosis. On 6 January 1925, he wrote to his mother: "The words "pain" and "suffering" which you use seem quite odd to me. A condition into which one has slithered gradually, and consequently got used to, is not suffering but simply a—condition. A condition that leaves room for joy and suffering like any other. A Homeric god might see human life only in terms of pain and suffering. This notion is as false as yours. . . . And I dare not think how [things] would be without Edith [his wife]. The great helper who turns suffering into difficulties, and the little comforter [Rafael, his son] who turns the rest into joy, are what have come of five years ago today [his engagement day]. And despite everything, the three of us, I, Edith, and Rafael, praise the day." (In Glatzer, *Franz Rosenzweig: His Life and Thought,* 142–43)

19. *Star,* see page 174.

20. Paul Mendes-Flohr, "Nationalism as a Spiritual Sensibility: The Philosophical Suppositions of Buber's Hebrew Humanism," in *Divided Passions: Jewish Intellectuals and the Experience of Modernity* (Detroit: Wayne State Univ. Press, 1991), 185.

21. "Urzelle des Stern der Erlösung: Brief an Rudolf Ehrenberg vom 18.11.1917" [Germ cell of the *Star of Redemption:* Letter to R.E. of 18 November 1917], in *Zweistromland,* 132. Rudolf Ehrenberg (1884–1969) was a medical professor at Göttingen.

22. The discussions and views with regard to Eastern and Asian philosophies and religions in the *Star* are both colored by the times and problematic in themselves. Robert Gibbs, in his *Correlations in Rosenzweig and Levinas* (Princeton, N.J.: Princeton Univ. Press, 1992), makes bold mention of Rosenzweig's failings in the *Star's* system of philosophy. "The two most flagrant claims are 1) that Judaism exists outside of history, and 2) that Christianity is spreading and must continue to spread over the whole world. . . . But the failure of Rosenzweig's system is more pervasive, because throughout *The Star of Redemption* Rosenzweig has not taken history half seriously enough. His accounts of Greece, China, and India in Part I seem barely historical, while his constant use of Islam in Part II reflects an embarrassing prejudice. In short, it seems that every time Rosenzweig tries to make any claim on the basis of historical facts, he is at best half-right; his empirical claims are false. For many social theorists that pretty well ends this chapter; indeed, it causes one to doubt the worth of this book as a whole" (p. 113). Gibbs does value the *Star,* and from here moves on with a helpful discussion of idealist readings of the historical record (pp. 114–16). Cf., pp. 96, 122, 138, and 266n.16.

Specific attention to Rosenzweig's treatment of Islam is given by Shlomo Pines's "Der Islam im 'Stern der Erlösung.' Eine Untersuchung zu Tendenzen und Quellen Franz Rosenzweigs," in *Hebräische Beiträge zur Wissenschaft des Judentums, deutsch angezeigt,* Jahrgang

3–5/1987–89 (Heidelberg: Verlag Lambert Schneider), 138–48. Pines's opening paragraph reads: "I shall try to demonstrate in this essay that a substantial part, perhaps indeed the majority of Rosenzweig's statements in the *Star of Redemption* concerning Islam were written in relation to and in discussion with the sections in Hegel's writings which also deal with the theme 'Islam.' Likewise it seems to me that Rosenzweig at times (without making explicit reference to this) uses the *Vorträge über den Islam* [*Lectures on Islam*] by Goldziher, which had appeared in 1910, shortly before the *Star of Redemption,* in order to get as it were a factual backing for his standpoint. Occasionally this happens, wittingly or unwittingly, in a more tendentious manner from a simplification of history and of religious reality."

23. Rosenzweig's dissertation, "Hegel und der Staat," of 1912 at Freiburg, under the supervision of Meinecke, was expanded and completed after the war. It was published in two volumes, interestingly, in the same year as the *Star,* 1920, under the assistance of the Heidelberg Akademie der Wissenschaften (Munich and Berlin: Verlag R. Oldenbourg). A planned second edition of 1937 was destroyed by the Gestapo.

24. *B & T,* 903. Friedrich Hölderlin (1770–1843) was an exquisitely fine German poet whom Rosenzweig especially admired. For one thing, he credits Hölderlin with being the first one successfully to translate Greek meter into the German language. See Glatzer, *Franz Rosenzweig: His Life and Thought,* 101.

25. *B & T,* 969.

26. Michael D. Oppenheim has addressed this issue in "The Relevance of Rosenzweig in the Eyes of His Israeli Critics," *Modern Judaism,* 7, no. 2 (May 1987), 193–206. He writes: "Despite the very positive way that commentators present Rosenzweig's writings on Jewish education and religious practice, many severely criticize him for believing that a real return to the tradition was possible in the

diaspora. Ehud Luz's comment about Rosenzweig's work in the field of Jewish education, while typical, is extremely powerful. He characterizes Rosenzweig as an aristocratic intellectual who overvalues the life of an individual or community. Luz, like others, insists that a whole Jewish framework of cultural and political life is the necessary pre-requisite for such a transformation" (199). While for many reasons much admired, Rosenzweig's "critics find it impossible to take seriously [his] claim that offsetting this renunciation of an active role in history, the eternal people are guaranteed protection from history's terrors. Their response obviously springs out of the dual experiences of death in the Holocaust 'kingdom' and life within the Jewish state" (203).

27. Of particular note is Emil Fackenheim. See *To Mend the World* (New York: Schocken, 1982).

28. "Blessed are you." God is spoken to in prayer, not about.

29. See Rosenzweig's Note to the poem by Jehuda Halevi, "Der Lohn" [Reward], in the Nijhoff edition, 109–11.

30. Paul Mendes-Flohr, "*Realpolitik* or Ethical Nationalism?" in *Divided Passions,* 171.

31. See the *Star,* 233.

32. Paul Mendes-Flohr, "Ambivalent Dialogue: Jewish-Christian Theological Encounter in the Weimar Republic," in *Divided Passions,* 136.

33. Glatzer, *Franz Rosenzweig: His Life and Thought,* 95–96.

34. Ibid., 97.

35. Ibid., 355.

36. Ibid., 157–58.

37. At the time of writing "The New Thinking," Rosenzweig had published the first edition of his translations of and notes to the Halevi poetry. This edition of 1924 (Konstanz: Oskar Wöhrle) included 60 hymns and poems. In 1927 he published an expanded edition comprising 92 (Lambert Schneider). Rosenzweig's son,

Rafael, edited the third edition, published in 1983 (The Hague: Martinus Nijhoff). At the time of Rosenzweig's death in 1929, he himself had had plans for a third edition of 103 hymns and poems. An English translation of Rosenzweig's Halevi book, with five chapters of commentary by the translator, is available: Barbara Ellen Galli, *Franz Rosenzweig and Jehuda Halevi: Translating, Translations and Translators* (Montreal: McGill-Queen's Univ. Press, 1995).

38. Nahum Glatzer, *Franz Rosenzweig: His Life and Thought.*

39. Reprinted in *Franz Rosenzweig: Der Mensch und Sein Werk: Gesammelte Schriften,* vol. 3, *Zweistromland: Kleinere Schriften zu Glauben und Denken* (The Hague: Martinus Nijhoff, 1984), 845. My translation.

40. *Star,* 97–105.

41. See the *Star,* 105–6.

42. Rosenzweig had written an unusual little book, called *Das Büchlein vom gesunden und kranken Menschenverstand.* It was an alternative presentation of his "healthy-minded" speech-thinking philosophy, a sort of philosophical novel, or play by way of letters, intended to address and to convey "commonsense" thinking in a less dense way than a system (*Star*) could do. He withdrew it from the printers, however, just before it was to be published. All editions are posthumous.

43. See *Star,* 106–11.

44. Translated in Glatzer, *Franz Rosenzweig: His Life and Thought,* 104. Original printed in *B & T,* 725.

45. *B & T,* 718.

46. Wendell S. Dietrich, "Franz Rosenzweig: Recent Works in French," in *Religious Studies Review* 13, no. 2 (April 1987), 99.

47. A very astute and interesting paper, "Eugen Rosenstock-Huessy (1888–1973) & Mikhail Bakhtin (1895–1975): Speech, the Spirit, and Social Change," dealing with the substance and thrust of the times in a comparative study of the European and the Russian

contexts, was presented by Harold M. Stahmer on 14 May 1993, at the Cracoviense Collegium Maximum Societatis Jesu in Cracow, Poland, at the invitation of its Rector, Dr. Adam Zak, S.J., and sponsored by The Transnational East-West Institute. Professor Stahmer read earlier versions of this paper at the 1992 Dartmouth College Conference on "The Renewal of Russian Spiritual Life: Its Relation to the Emergence of Democratic Institutions," and in March 1993 in Moscow, Russia, at a Conference on "Russian Philosophy and the Russia of Today."

48. Paul Mendes-Flohr, "Scholarship as a Craft: Reflections on the Legacy of Nahum Glatzer," *Modern Judaism* 13 (1993); 274.

49. Ibid., 274–75. Mendes-Flohr is quoting from a letter Rosenzweig wrote to Eugen Rosenstock-Huessy, undated, in E. Rosenstock-Huessy, ed., *Judaism Despite Christianity: The "Letters on Christianity and Judaism" between Eugen Rosenstock-Huessy and Franz Rosenzweig,* trans. Dorothy Emmet (Tuscaloosa: Univ. of Alabama Press, 1969), 168.

50. *Der Jude: Eine Monatsschrift,* vol. 6 (Berlin: Jüdischer Verlag, 1921/22), 259–64. An English translation (by Joachim Neugroschel) appears under the title, "Franz Rosenzweig's *The Star of Redemption* (A Review)," in *The Jew: Essays from Martin Buber's Journal, Der Jude, 1916–1918,* selected, edited, and introduced by Arthur A. Cohen (Tuscaloosa: Univ. of Alabama Press and Jewish Publication Society of America, 1980), 273–85. See pages 133–49 of the present volume.

51. "Denn Name, ist nicht Schall und Rauch, sondern Wort und Feuer. Den Namen gilt es zu nennen und zu bekommen: ich glaub' ihn" [*Stern,* 209]. In the William Hallo translation (p. 188), the English is as follows: "For name is in truth word and fire, and not sound and fury as unbelief would have it again and again in obstinate vacuity. It is incumbent to name the name and to acknowledge: I believe it" (*The Star of Redemption* [Notre Dame: Notre Dame Univ. Press,

1985]). In *The Jew* (p. 273) it reads: "A name is not sound and smoke, it is word and fire. The name must be named and professed: I believe in it."

52. *B & T, 2. Band 1918–1929,* 752.

53. "In the book I only regret . . . the unnecessary word of the end with which the author concludes and in which he also pays tribute to our times and in that he also suddenly enjoins in the call: "*from philosophy to life,*" he who surely does not need to speak in this way."

54. *B & T, 2. Band 1918–1929,* 735–36.

2. "Germ Cell" of *The Star of Redemption*

1. "Man is the measure of all things."
2. "God and His Word are the measure of all things."
3. "A thinking of thinking."
4. See Johann Wolfgang von Goethe, *Faust,* Part 2, line 4727.
5. "Recollection."
6. "Matter."
7. "Looking to you."

3. "The New Thinking": A Few Supplemental Remarks to the *Star*

1. *Zeitwort* is the German term for *verb.* [Tr.]
2. *Zeit* connotes both tense (*Tempus*) and *time.* [Tr.].

4. The Exodus from Philosophy

1. The reference is to the other three books covered in Susman's review, and omitted here: Georg Simmel's *Lebenanschauung,* Oswald Spengler's *Untergang des Abendlandes,* and Ernst Bloch's *Geist der Utopie.*

6. *The Star of Redemption*

1. *Hegel und der Staat* (München und Berlin: Verlag R. Olden-bourg, 1920).

2. "Against the philosophers," the motto of book 1 of the *Star* [Tr.].

3. "Against the theologians," the motto of book 2 of the *Star* [Tr.].

4. "Against the tyrants," the motto of book 3 of the *Star* [Tr.].

9. Retracing the Steps of Franz Rosenzweig

1. Friedrich Wilhelm Joseph von Schelling, *On the History of Modern Philosophy,* trans. Andrew Bowie (Cambridge: Cambridge Univ. Press, 1994), 64.

2. "Franz Rosenzweig und die Akademie für die Wissenschaft des Judentums," in *Jüdische Wochenzeitung für Kassel, Hessen und Waldeck,* 13 December 1929, p. 2.

3. *Critique of Pure Reason,* trans. Norman Kemp Smith (New York: St. Martin's Press, 1965), Axi–xii. [Emphasis added.] The disclosure of the *topos* of the *new* is thus at once brought within the limit of law. The question of freedom implicit here, belongs in an essential way to a truly given account of thinking and its origin. "On the Essence of Truth," in Martin Heidegger, *Basic Writings,* ed. David Farrell Krell (New York: Harper & Row, 1977), 138–39. It is, thereby, a measure of the new thinking, both insofar as it reviews the old, and insofar as it views itself.

4. Ibid., Axiia.

5. See Abbreviations on page 152 for specific key.

6. Leo Strauss, *Spinoza's Critique of Religion,* trans. E. M. Sinclair (New York: Schocken Books, 1965), 178–82.

7. Ibid., 15. Emphasis added.

8. "On the Uses and Disadvantages of History for Life," section 10, in *Untimely Meditations,* trans. R. J. Hollingdale (Cambridge: Cambridge Univ. Press, 1983), 117.

9. "'It looks to me as though the investigation we are undertaking is no ordinary thing, but one for a man who sees sharply. Since we're not clever men,' I said, 'in my opinion we should make this kind of investigation of it: if someone had, for example, ordered men who don't see very sharply to read little letters from afar and then someone had the thought that the same letters are somewhere else also, but bigger and in a bigger place, I suppose it would look like a godsend to be able to consider the little ones after having read these first, if, of course, they do happen to be the same [368c–d].'" *The Republic of Plato,* trans. Allan Bloom (New York: Basic Books, 1968).

10. This necessity is philosophically constituted by the temporal distance that is revealed in the philosopher who, "*necessarily* as a man of tomorrow and the day after tomorrow, has always found himself, and *had* to find himself, in contradiction to his today: his enemy every time was the ideal of today."[a] It is the task or mission of the philosopher [#203], of the one who is the distance into which man in some future may be brought to pass, to further [*fördern*] or distance man [#211]. The philosopher is the demand or the summons [*Forderung*] for the violence without which the new, distant time and the man of that time cannot be realized. Nietzsche is the revolutionary tribunal before which must pass those "eternal values" that, in their eternal aspect, are to be overcome [#203]; and, too, the philosophers who are, and who have been—the undistant ones, who, with "their lack of historical sense," and "their hatred of the very idea [*Vorstellung*] of becoming," placed themselves in the service of those values.[b] The Nietzschean tribunal brings to a radical and revolutionary end that which seemed complete in the Kantian age, "truly [*eigentlich*] the age of critique [Axiia]": now—

"*Genuine (eigentliche) philosophers are commanders and lawgivers. . . .*
With a creative hand they grasp [*greifen*] at the future, and everything, what is and what was, becomes thereby for them a means,
an instrument, a hammer." The will in its infinite expression is present in the very way in which the hand grasps at that which is not
yet: in its instrumental extension of itself. The silence of power as
the mediation of self and nature replaces, thereby, the mediation
of soul and *cosmos* by speech. The form of touch, supplemented by
the illimitable apparatus of *technē*, replaces the form of seeing[c]—and
therewith the way in which philosophy is conceived with respect
to distance: it is no longer the distance of looking at the eternal
whole;[d] it is, in place of this, the distance into which that which
is not yet is to be brought forth by the effort and exercise of creative will. It is over this distance-bearing transvaluation of values that
the philosophers on the Nietzschean tribunal preside—"Their
'knowing' is a *creating,* their creating is a legislation, their will to
truth is—*will to power* [#211]"—and take to its unthought end the
work of the Kantian court. That is to say, the freedom and openness that are the marks of the critical examination [*freie und öffentliche
Prüfung* (Axiia)] by which reason establishes its supremacy as judge
will be made to pass in turn before that higher tribunal for which
the free and open are the attributes of existence itself. Nietzsche is
the summons to *Geist* to step forward into the eventuation of the
distant, future furthering of man. Whether or not an adequate account can be given of this event of the free and open, is the question on which both existentialism and the postmodern project may
be said to stand or fall.[e]

   a. Friedrich Nietzsche, *Beyond Good and Evil,* #211.

   b. Friedrich Nietzsche, *Twilight of the Idols,* "Reason in Philosophy," #1.

   c. The degradation of seeing is corollary to the apotheosis of creativity: distance as the place of doing *qua* making—of that which is the new, or newly begun, and hence that which has its cause outside itself; c1 in it there is neither that which is last [*eschaton*] nor that which is end [*telos*].c2 Distance ceases to be the resting place to which seeing *qua* thinking looks—for there is nothing in the distance. There is no Edenic "key permitting one to enter places the gates to which were locked"—such that "when these gates are opened and these places are entered into, the souls will find rest therein, the eyes will be delighted, and the bodies will be eased of their toil and of their labor."c3 Rather, distance is the actuality of will's creative inauguration, its shaping hand— or embodiment. It is produced out of the corporeal proximity of touch. It is the nature of proximity that only the part can be perceived; it is the nature of touch that that which is perceived is present in the form of a covering or concealment.c4 These containments ultimately are seen within the economy of liberation. That which is whole, and that which comes to light within the provenance of its optic, are given to the soul; and it is from the narrow confinements of the soul, into the free and open distance, that that which is the furthering of man must go: "[the] real, non-corporal soul is not a substance, it is the element in which are articulated the effects of a certain type of power and the reference of a certain type of knowledge, the machinery by which the power relations give rise to a possible corpus of knowledge, and knowledge extends and reinforces the effects of this power. . . . the soul is the prison of the body."c5

c.1. Modernity is concentrated into the distance that separates soul and self. The project of the self has as its horizon coming-to-be. In this respect, the Cartesian deduction of the *cogitata* from the *ego cogitans* and the essays of the authorial "I" in Montaigne are essentially related. Each is an example of the conjunction of heterology and autonomy that structures the modern self-understanding. The autonomy of modern political self-understanding displays this conjunction with reference to both providence and nature. Cf. Leo Strauss, *Thoughts on Machiavelli* (Seattle: Univ. of Washington Press, 1969), 198–99, 297.

c.2. *Twilight,* #4.

c.3. *The Guide for the Perplexed,* trans. Shlomo Pines (Chicago: Univ. of Chicago Press, 1963), 20 ("Introduction to the First Part," 12a).

c.4. On touch as transimmanent, v. Jean Luc-Nancy, *The Muses,* trans. Peggy Kamuf (Stanford: Stanford Univ. Press, 1996), 16–20.

c.5. Michel Foucault, *Discipline and Punish,* trans. Alan Sheridan (New York: Vintage Books, 1979), 29–30.

d. "The difficulty inherent in the philosophy of the will to power led after Nietzsche to the explicit renunciation of the very notion of eternity. Modern thought reaches its culmination, its highest self-consciousness, in the most radical historicism, i.e., in explicitly condemning to oblivion the notion of eternity. For oblivion of eternity, or, in other words, estrangement from man's deepest desire and therewith from the primary issues, is the price which modern man had to pay, from the very beginning, for attempting to be absolutely sovereign, to become the master and owner of nature, to conquer chance. Leo Strauss, "What is Political Philosophy?" in *What Is Political Philosophy?* (New York: Free Press, 1959), 55.

e. "The movement of Nietzsche's thought can be understood as a movement from the supremacy of history towards the supremacy of nature, a movement that *by-passes* the supremacy of reason. . . . Existentialism is the attempt to free Nietzsche's alleged overcoming of relativism from the consequences of his relapse into metaphysics or of his recourse to nature." Leo Strauss, "Relativism," in *The Rebirth of Classical Political Rationalism,* ed. Thomas L. Pangle (Chicago: Univ. of Chicago Press, 1989), 26. [Emphasis added.]

11. The paraphrase that follows is drawn from this account.

12. The depiction of ascent that follows throughout, along with the entire registry of terms for movement, the correlatives of place, their constitutive temporalities, and the horizon of distance within which they are set are to be thought of "ecstatically." Cf. Martin Heidegger, *Die Grundprobleme der Phänomenologie* (Frankfort-am-Main: Vittorio Klostermann, 1975), 380–81.

13. *Human, All-Too Human,* 2:#99.

14. And we, who think of happiness raising, / would feel the emotion / that almost dismays us / when a happy thing falls. Rainer Maria Rilke, "The Tenth Elegy," in *Duino Elegies.* Cf. *BG&E,* #205.

15. *Thus Spoke Zarathustra,* "Prologue."

16. "The scientific fields are quite diverse. The ways they treat their objects of inquiry differ fundamentally. Today only the technical organization of universities and faculties consolidates this burgeoning multiplicity of disciplines; the practical establishment of goals by each discipline provides the only meaningful source of unity. Nonetheless, the rootedness of the sciences in their essential ground has atrophied." "What is Metaphysics," in Martin Heidegger, *Basic Writings,* ed. David Farrell Krell (New York: Harper & Row, 1977), 96.

It is instructive to recall the similarity between Rosenzweig and Heidegger at this point, with a view to marking the essential ground that separates them.

17. *Untimely Meditations,* 117.

18. Rosenzweig's use of words built on the stem *eig-* conforms to the surface meanings of everyday usage. Beyond this, there is the deeper, that is, technical, connotation: the role that they play in the

idiom of idealist[a] and existentialist[b] thought (cf. 10). In this context, *das eig-* for Rosenzweig carries with it the deeper sense of a particularity or ownness that is irreducible to and unpossessable by totalizing rationality, or that rationality that defines for him the tradition of Western philosophy. On Rosenzweig's understanding of the latter,[c] the essential mark of *das eig-* is revealed in the *ti esti* (*was ist*) question—in the horizon of timelessness in which its asking takes place. What is lost in this substantivization of the actual is the seriality (*Folge*), "the stream of life [p. 30]," "the course of life" in which "our act is our act [p. 31]." Temporality is linked, thereby, in a particular determinative way to that which is narrational. This linkage in itself does not simply decide the difference between the *new thinking* and idealism.[d] Rather, it points to a kindredness wherein that determination may be more finely made.[e]

    a. In philosophy, Reason comes to know itself and deals only with itself so that its whole work and activity are grounded in itself, and with respect to the inner essence of philosophy there are neither predecessors nor successors.

    Nor is it any more correct to speak of *personal views* entertained in philosophy than of its steady improvement. How could the rational be a personal idiosyncrasy? (*Wie sollte das Vernünftige eigentümlich sein?*) Whatever is thus peculiar in a philosophy must *ipso facto* belong to the form of the system and not to the essence of the philosophy. If something idiosyncratic actually constituted the essence of a philosophy, it would not be a philosophy . . .

Georg Wilhelm Friedrich Hegel, *The Difference Between Fichte's and Schelling's System of Philosophy,* trans. H. S. Harris and Walter Cerf (New York: State Univ. of New York Press, 1977), 87.

    b. "We recognize the problem of system in the Idealists (the form of philosophizing as the true (*eigentliche*) crux of philosophy), but it doesn't dominate the form of our particular (*eigenen*) philosophizing as it does theirs; we don't want to be philosophers in that we philosophize, but *human beings,* and that being so, we must bring our philosophizing into the form of our humanity." Franz Rosenzweig to Eugen Rosenstock, in *Franz Rosenzweig/Briefe,* selected and edited by Edith Rosenzweig (Berlin: Schocken Verlag, 1935), 718. Hereafter: *Briefe.*

    c. *Das Büchlein vom gesunden und kranken Menschenverstand,* ed. Nahum Glatzer (Düsseldorf: Joseph Melzer Verlag, 1964), 28–33.

    d. Thus, Hegel writes of Reinhold: "His love of, and faith in, truth have risen to an elevation (*Höhe*) so pure and so sickening, that in order to found and ground the step (*Schritt*) into the temple properly (*recht*), Reinhold has built a spacious vestibule in which philosophy keeps itself so busy with analysis, with methodology and with storytelling (*Erzählen*), that it saves itself from taking the step altogether." *The Difference,* 88.

    e. "Telling a story in this metaleptic sense of the term is not a matter of choice. The story is the symbolic form the questioner has to adopt necessarily when he gives an account of his quest as the event of wresting, by the response of his human search to a divine movement, the truth of a reality from a reality pregnant with truth yet unrevealed. Moreover, the story remains the constant symbolism of the quest even when the tension between divine and human story is reduced to the zero of identity as in the dialectical story told by the self-identical *logos* of the Hegelian system." Eric Voegelin, *In Search of Order,* vol. 5 of *Order and History* (Baton Rouge: Louisiana State Univ. Press, 1987), 24.

19. Johann Wolfgang von Goethe, *Faust,* line 425.

20. Walter Benjamin, *The Origin of German Tragic Drama,* trans. John Osborne (London: NLB, 1977), 164–65.

21. The concentric paths along which Rosenzweig's suggestive

narrative moves cannot be followed further in this essay. It is instructive, nonetheless, to look in the direction of their course and, too, of those kindred to its *itinerarium*. Hitherto, all philosophical interest had moved around [*um . . . bewegt*] the knowable whole—philosophy repeats the movement of the object [*Gegenstand*] of its desire: *logos* mediates *cosmos* and *psuchē*. It knows [*wissen*] the human being only in his relation [*in seinem Verhältnis*] to this knowable whole. To know the human being in relation is to assimilate that which is unique and his own property [*der Einzige und sein Eigentum*] to the whole—it is to make the *unpossessable* other that is eccentric to the whole (that *as* other is thus *ec-centric*, that *as* ec-centric is thus unpossessable, that *as* knowable [*erkennbar*] is thus only in the exemplarity of the beyond) one with the whole. But man *as* other [*ein andres*], *as* the living one [*der lebendige Mensch*], steps forward [*trat*], unpossessably [*selbständig*]—over against [*gegenüber*] the knowable world. The syntactic standing against [*Gegenstand*] is transformed into the paratactic standing over [*gegenüber*], or beyond [*jenseits*]. The *stasis* of the circular (whole), is transcended by the *dunamis* of the linear (individual), the arcs of the circle by the lines of the star. It is this linearity that leads into life, into the *turning* of *Geist* that Rosenzweig opposes in the conclusion of the *Star* to the *return* of *Geist* with which Hegel's *Phenomenology* concludes.

22. Ferdinand Ebner, *Das Wort und die geistigen Realitäten* (Munich: Kösel Verlag, 1963), 269.

23. "Ethics and Spirit," in Emannuel Levinas, *Difficult Freedom: Essays on Judaism,* trans. Sean Hand (Baltimore: Johns Hopkins Univ. Press, 1990), 8.

24. *Der Tod ist* eigenste *Möglichkeit des Daseins.* Martin Heidegger, *Sein und Zeit* (Tübingen: Max Niemeyer Verlag, 1967), 263.

25. Martin Heidegger, *Schelling's Treatise on the Essence of Human Freedom,* trans. Joan Stambaugh (Ohio: Ohio Univ. Press, 1985), 2.

Cf. Theodor Adorno, *Against Epistemology,* trans. Willis Domingo (Oxford: Basil Blackwell, 1982), 16.

26. "Das Wesen des Menschen ist wesentlich seine eigne That." F.W.J. von Schelling, *Philosophische Untersuchungen über das Wesen der Menschen Freiheit und die damit zusammenhangenden Gegenstände,* in *Sämmtliche Werke,* vol. 7 (Stuttgart und Augsburg: J. G. Cotta'scher Verlag, 1860), 385.

Das eig-, for Rosenzweig, unfettered from the *Gesellschaft* of philosophy that had ascribed to thinking oneness [*Einheit*] and to being allness [*Allheit*] (4/1:18), is the place of freedom's actualization. Into this place the living man stepped [*trat* (4/1:14)]; along its way went [*ging* (4/1:15)] the student. Terms of movement such as these signify, in the passages considered, the condition of health and infirmity at the event [*Ereignis*] of freedom. Their signification derives structurally from the work's composition. It is only in view of that composition that the terms can be properly interpreted. *The Star of Redemption* belongs to the genre of the spiritual quest. It is a topology of the soul's *itinerarium.* In Rosenzweig's hands, the genre incorporates what he sees as the marks distinctive of biblical narrative:

"In certain circumstances, moreover, a [biblical] story is framed around a whole series of similar or formally linked words or formulaic sentences, which hold together, each with that which follows it, like the exchanges of repartee [*schlagfertiger Dialog*]. These are distinguished, precisely by the importance of the *sequence* in which they appear, from the regular epithets and formulaically recurring sentences of Homeric epic, which they might at first superficially resemble. The epithets and the formulae of epic give the poem a unified coloration, which like all visual things should be perceived in a single, comprehensive view; the recurring components of biblical narrative cannot be so viewed, but must rather be perceived in sequence; and where a story or a group of stories is ordered around a recurring formula, the formula must sound more portentous, more richly orchestrated, at each recurrence."[a]

Rosenzweig employs a number of key words and formulaic expressions in the sequence of the work's itinerary. Certain terms of posture and movement fit this pattern. Thus, the overall movement of the work is conveyed by the figurations of *stehen, hinanschreiten,* and *wandeln,* in which its three *parts* respectively culminate:

> Wir stehen an dem Übergang,—dem Übergang des Geheimnisses in das Wunder (*"Übergang"* [7/1:118]).
> We *stand* at the overpass—the overpass of the mystery into miracle.

> Wir schreiten hinan über die Schwelle der Überwelt, die Schwelle vom Wunder zur Erleuchtung (*"Schwelle"* [7/2:223]).
> We *step* upward over the threshold of the overworld, the threshold from miracle to illumination.

> Einfältig wandeln mit deinem Gott—die worte stehen über dem Tor, dem Tor, das aus dem geheimnisvoll-wunderbaren Leuchten des göttlichen Heiligtums. . . . herausführt. . . . INS LEBEN (*"Tor"* [7/3: 211].
> To *walk on* simply with your God—the words stand over the gate, the gate that leads out of the mystery filled—wonderful radiance of the divine sanctuary. . . . INTO LIFE.

At the same time, the idiom of the work may be seen to reflect the sequence and progression of its quest. The depictions of *Geist* as *Kletterer,* or philosophy as *lahm* (8:133), must be measured by reference to the path along which the book as a whole moves.

a. Franz Rosenzweig, "The Secret of Biblical Narrative Form," in Martin Buber and Franz Rosenzweig, *Scripture and Translation,* trans. Lawrence Rosenwald with Everett Fox (Bloomington: Indiana Univ. Press, 1994), 135.

27. "The Other is not only known, he is greeted. He is not only named, but also invoked. To put it in grammatical terms, the Other does not appear in the nominative, but in the vocative." "Ethics and Spirit," 7.

28. The distinction is critical:

concreteness in the analysis of the Dasein phenomena, which give direction and content to Dasein's metaphysical projection, easily misleads one, first, into taking the concrete phenomena of Dasein by themselves and, second, into taking them as existentiell absolutes in their extreme, fundamental-ontological conceptualization. The more radical the existentiell involvement, the more concrete the ontological-metaphysical project. But the more concrete this interpretation of Dasein is, the easier it becomes to misunderstand in principle by taking the existentiell involvement for the single most important thing, whereas this involvement, itself becomes manifest in the project, with all its indifference to the particularity of the person.

Martin Heidegger, *The Metaphysical Foundations of Logic,* trans. Michael Heim (Bloomington: Indiana Univ. Press, 1984), 140.

Rosenzweig's *Denken* expresses the pull of these tendencies. The present reading is intended to bring out the topology underlying that expression, the access to which is blocked by the conventional existential readings.

29. "It is God's will to universalize everything, to lift it to unity with light or to preserve it therein; but the will of the deep is to particularize everything or to make it creature-like. It wishes dif-

ferentiation only so that identity may become evident to itself and to the will of the deep." F.W.J. von Schelling, *Of Human Freedom,* trans. James Gutman (Chicago: Open Court Publishing, 1936), 58–59. [*Sämmtliche Werke,* vol. 7, s. 381–82].

30. The structure of the *calling-forth* is anticipatory. That which it evokes is for the sake of that which is to be given to the one who waits. What passes between God and the human being at this point, however, has a deeper structure than the sense of the futural conventionally denotes—for God's love has always been in advance of every commandment, as the "Here am I" must be in advance of every observance.

31. On the question of *eidos,* cf. Eric Voegelin, *The New Science of Politics* (Chicago: Univ. of Chicago Press), 119ff; Thomas Prufer, "Providence and Imitation: Sophocles' *Oedipus Rex* and Aristotle's *Poetics,*" in *Recapitulations* (Washington, D.C.: Catholic Univ. Press of America, 1993), 12–21.

32. *Das Büchlein,* 28–33.

33. The narrative account of the call-to philosophical man, in effect the story of an *Eingang,* tells of the way in which the old thinking is surpassed by the new. The story of the call-to man, which belongs as well to the *genre* of *Eingang,* tells of the way in which the old thinking is surpassed by faith. Through their conflation, the question of Athens and Jerusalem is absorbed into a version of the quarrel between the ancients and the moderns, that is, the question of the relationship between philosophy and faith is transposed into the distinction between the old and the new thinking. The change in the conception of philosophy, faith, and hence of their relationship, that results effectively from this transposition conceals the fundamentality[a] of the Athens-Jerusalem question—a fundamentality that may be recovered by turning to Maimonides' parallel account (*The Guide for the Perplexed,* 1:2), in which the distinction is made in terms of theoretical and practical virtue. As a consequence of this

concealment, the *new thinking* is threatened with the loss not only of the ground from which to radically question itself, but, as well, the means without which the way back to that soul-turning ground is given over wholly, as the *Republic* teaches, to chance and what is divine. "At this moment, the sectarian is born."[b]

a. "One cannot recall too often this remark of Goethe . . . 'Das eigentliche, einzige und tiefste Thema der Welt- und Menschengeschichte, dem alle übrigen untergeordnet sind, bleibt der Konflikt des Unglaubens und Glaubens.'" [The *eigentliche, einzige* and deepest theme of world and human history, that to which all additional ones are subordinated, remains the conflict of unbelief and belief.] Leo Strauss, "The Law of Reason in the *Kuzari,*" in *Persecution and the Art of Writing* (Glencoe, Ill.: Free Press, 1952), 107, n. 35.

b. Leo Strauss, *On Tyranny* (New York: The Free Press of Glencoe, 1963), 210. Cf. *The Guide,* 292 (2. 15. 33b): "passions get the better of all sects, even of the philosophers." On the *thumos* that infuses sectarianism, cf. *The Guide,* 66 (1:31. 34b), and Saint Augustine, *Confessions,* 12. 25. (34); on the form of its appearance in the beginning of modern philosophy, cf. Joseph Pieper, *Leisure the Basis of Culture,* trans. Alexander Dru (New York: Mentor-Omega Books, 1963), 98–111.

34. These stories complement each other in accordance with particular emplotments. What is literal in one account may appear figuratively in another, without thereby affecting the synonymies. Thus, the philosopher is portrayed as refusing to enter the flow of life. His withdrawal takes the form of a standing stock still (cf. 5:149), or the lameness that is the mark of the philosopher (8:133). The man who is his complement has refused to enter into the place of questioning—"the question concerning the you remains mere question" [*Die Frage nach dem Du bleibt blosse Frage* (7/2:113)]. He remains still in the silence wherein he hides. Both philosopher and

man hide—but not simply in some place; they hide within the *place-taking* [*an der Stelle*] as such—the place-taking whose borders constitute the *Schwelle*, and thus may be seen from both sides: *So hat er [der Philosoph] nun auch an der Stelle, wo sonst der Fluss des Lebens flosse, das Standbild des Gegenstands*[a]); *An Stelle des unbestimmten . . . tritt der Vokativ, der Anruf* (7/2: 113).

   a. *Das Büchlein*, 30.

35. *Das Büchlein*, 30.

36. The same complementarity obtains, that is, the same form is evident, in the matter of Rosenzweig's account of Jewish existence: the *call-to* the safe and undisturbed little corner [*ein sicheres, ungestörtes Eckchen* (3:497)] in which it has removed itself from the flow of passing life [*das Leben flutet unbekümmert daran vorüber* (3:497)]; trust [*Vertrauen*] as the condition for its *Eingang*; readiness [*Bereitschaft*] into which it is called-forth. The *calling-forth* for the sake of learning concentrates the parallels—a dead booklearning [*tote Buchgelehrsamkeit* (3:497)] restricted [*eingeschränkt*] to the poverty of a few fundamental concepts [*Grundbegriffe* (2:702)]: the philosopher confined to essentiality [*beschränkt auf das Eigentliche*].[a] The measure of the technical weight that the language may be made to bear is Rosenzweig's assertion that Jewish being is not a limit [*Judesein ist kein Schranke* (3:493)].

   a. *Das Büchlein*, 32.

37. *The Difference*, 88.

38. Diese Logik ist nicht zeitlos. Im Gegenteil. Sie ist die Logik des wirklichen, also zeitlichen Erkennens.

Nämlich: Ich wurde genannt.

Ich spreche.

Ich werde Antwort erhalten.

Zwischen diesen Zeiten geschieht alles Erkennen. Ist das Wissen? oder Glauben? Sie sehen jedenfalls eins: hier gilt kein Misstrauen. Hier leben Sie vom Vertrauen. (1:603)

39. "Eingang"—Wer du auch seist: am Abend tritt hinaus / aus deiner Stube, drin du alles weisst; als letztes vor der Ferne liegt dein Haus: / wer du auch seist.

40. "So—now you will know why I think in individuals (I prefer to say in men) and not in 'branches.' That these men are each one the whole, . . . [is a] fundamental truth." *Briefe,* 713.

41. Nichts Geringeres fragt die Zeit den Menschen von heut als: Wer bist du? wer willst du sein? du als ganzer Mensch, nicht zu einem Teil deines Wesens. (4:419)

42. "The *vita contemplativa* requires a turning around of the whole soul, but that does not mean that one can understand the *vita contemplativa* adequately in respect of its effects on the (if you forgive the expression) nontheoretical part of the soul.

> The closest classical equivalent of 'existential' is 'practical,' insofar as one understands practical in contradistinction to 'theoretical.' Existentialist philosophy will perhaps appear at some time in the future as the paradoxical effort to lead the thought of the praxis of the practical to its, in my mind, absurd last consequences. Under these conditions praxis ceases indeed to be actually praxis and transforms itself into 'existence.' . . . to the rejection of theory in the name of a praxis that is no longer intelligible as praxis."[a]

Theoria, which cannot truly be understood apart from death—or, more exactly, the freedom from the fear of death (*Republic,* 486a–b)—bears death along with it as a surplus that carries over into its rejection. For Rosenzweig, in the name of existence, the rejection assumes the form of the death of the *self;* for Levinas, in the name of *praxis,* it is the death of the *other*—the fear of death suffered, and the fear of violent death enacted,[b] respectively. Levinas's advance upon the pathos of Rosenzweig's thought may be argued along the following lines: the *praxis* of death raises the question of virtue in a way in which its sheer facticity does not; for the question of virtue cannot be raised adequately without at the same time raising the question of the order or rank of the virtues, and thereby the question of the highest virtue.[c] Levinas thus preserves—albeit attenuatedly—the question of the relationship of intellectual and practical virtue. That question, however, is identical with the question of the *lives* in which these virtues are preeminently manifested: the *bios theoretikos* and the *bios praktikos*. The rejection of *theoria*, then, can no longer give an account of itself simply based on the view of philosophy as a system. Insofar as the question of philosophy now must be raised anew, there is no certainty that it has come to an end, or that its rejection is called for compellingly.

a. Leo Strauss to Eric Voegelin, in *Faith and Political Philosophy: The Correspondence Between Leo Strauss and Eric Voegelin, 1934–1964,* trans. and ed. by Peter Emberley and Barry Cooper (University Park: Pennsylvania State Univ. Press, 1993), 65–66.

b. The matter of death needs to be thought beyond the limits of its appearance in both Rosenzweig and Levinas. The death of the self, and the temptation to murder that arises in the face of the other along with the inscription of the impossibility of its enactment, are framed by an exigency that places it in the domain of the necessary. It is in the domain of that which is more free, that is, the domain of virtue that, while including justice, points beyond it, that the matter of death comes most pressingly upon us in the form of a horrible enemy (*atrocissimam inimicam*)[b1]—that is to say, in the death of the *philos*.[b2] For all this, in considering the matter of death in relation to the philosophical life, it remains critical that one be mindful of the way in which the discussion of friendship in the closing books of the *Nicomachean Ethics* points to that life and in its turn is superseded by it.

b.1. Saint Augustine, *Confessions,* 4. 6 (11).

b.2. the consideration of one's own death is surpassed by the consideration of the death of a loved one.

It is at this point that I am most radically opposed not only to Heidegger and Sartre but to most earlier philosophers as well. One notable exception ought to be mentioned, and, as so often, it is Schelling. . . .

Gabriel Marcel, "My Death," in *Tragic Wisdom and Beyond,* trans. Stephen Jolin and Peter McCormick (Evanston, Ill.: Northwestern Univ. Press, 1973), 131.

    c. *BG&E*, 1.17.

43. It is instructive to compare *Theætetus,* 173c–176a with *Das Wort,* 119. That comparison, taken in conjunction with the exchange that follows next in the *Theætetus* (and what would follow from it on comparison with Schelling's consideration of this matter in *Of Human Freedom*), makes it possible to see certain essential questions that must be asked of the new thinking.

44. "On the higher [*höheren*] Man (#14)," in *Thus Spoke Zarathustra: Fourth and Last Part.*

45. The topology of the *Eingang* remains here within the outlines of a question: that of the place of philosophy's *archē*. No geographical or historical designation is able to give an account of this. The place of thinking is primordially anterior to that in which it takes place. It is the West that sets in its place. It does not follow, thereby, that the place of thinking—which remains throughout *archē*—is a metaphor. The question of representation cannot be answered in advance of the actuality of seeing: "but the philosopher, devoted to the look [*idea*] of that which is always through calculations [*logismon*], it's on account of the brilliance of the place [*choras*—i.e., the place that is proper, *eigentlich,* to it] that he's in no way easy to be seen, for the eyes of the soul of the many are incapable of keeping up a steady gaze on the divine (*Soph.* 254a–b)."[a] The question of metaphor (*meta-*

phorein/carrying across: *Poetics,* 1457b), then, remains in this case undecidable in advance of a crossing over or going-in to thinking. On Rosenzweig's account, thinking, thereby, repeats the movement of existing or living in which thinking itself was surpassed. *Weltanschauung* steps forward over against [*tritt gegenüber*] *Lebenanschauung*—but to this different, distantiated, end: That which had always been present in singularity, and whose presence yet remains as an inexpungeable trace within the "realm of the world knowing" [*Bereich des Weltwissens*], is brought within the construction of, that is, under the conceptuality of, the old thinking's *geistig* mastery—and, thereby, within its violence.[b] In narrating this repetition, that is, in giving an account of the beginning of philosophy, Rosenzweig draws attention to that which it first laid claim to [*beanspruchte*]: "to be the *All.*" This *All,* Rosenzweig observes, "is the subject of the first sentence [*Satz*] that philosophy had spoken at its birth." This sentence is a sign of the lameness or deformity of its condition (8:133), of the way in which it comes into the world.[c] This sign is revealed in that which Rosenzweig hears in it: "In that first sentence of philosophy, the 'All is water,' there is already hidden the presupposition of the world's conceivability [*Denkbarkeit*], even if Parmenides first expressly stated the identity of being and thinking" (7/1:18). Rosenzweig discloses, thereby, the origin of thinking by identifying the presupposition that it bears within it. This disclosure, however, fails to give an account of the *archē* of thinking. The hidden within thinking that is thoughtfully brought to light, is itself accounted for by entering the place of thinking—for it remains always and only the hiddenness of thinking. The path *vom Nichts zum Etwas* (7/1:33) that Rosenzweig follows throughout the course of *The Star of Redemption* is not entered upon where he turns to the question of thinking. Rather, that question is taken up into or placed within tradition—the tradition, as he denominates it, from Ionia to Jena. Rosenzweig, in the end, understands thinking under the aspect of the history of thought. Irrespective of the substance of that understanding, it is this move to tradition as such, to the *topos* upon which philosophy is no longer a questioning—hence, no longer *philo-sophia*—that is decisive.[d] That is to say, he understands the high in terms of the low.

a. *The Being of the Beautiful: Plato's Theatetus, Sophist, and Statesman,* trans. Seth Benardete (Chicago: Univ. of Chicago Press, 1984).

b. The aggravation of violence is evident in the passage from Rosenzweig to Levinas: from the action of a defiance [*er-trotzen* (7/1:18)] to the temptation to murder [*la tentation du meurtre*]. The aggravation lies in the temptation, as such: in the mediation of a phantasm, even the suggestion of *réssentiment*. Corresponding to the violence of this change in what is perceived as thinking's desire, is the violent desire for *l'expérience limitée* of life. "Ethics and Spirit," 8.

c. The implicit word-play on *Satz* [sentence, leap] can be assumed in Rosenzweig's depiction of philosophy as *lahm*. Cf. Martin Heidegger, *The Principle of Reason,* trans. Reginald Lilly (Bloomington: Indiana Univ. Press, 1991), 50–53.

d. Philosophy "als tradiertes ja kein Fragen mehr ist." Leo Strauss to Gerhard Krüger, November 17, 1932.

46. The Buber-Rosenzweig translation of *Gen.* 2:6 reads "aus der Erde stieg da ein Dunst."

47. *Das Wort,* 121–22.

48. "One-Way Street," in Walter Benjamin, *Reflections,* trans. Edmund Jephcott (New York: Harcourt Brace Jovanovich, 1978), 81.

49. *Das Büchlein,* 32.

50. "The manner of study in ancient times is distinct from that of the modern world, in that the former consisted in the cultivation and perfecting of the natural mind. Testing life carefully at all points, philosophizing about everything it came across, the former created an experience permeated through and through by universals. In

modern times, however, the individual finds the abstract form ready made. . . . Hence nowadays the task before us consists not so much in getting the individual clear of the stage of sensuous immediacy, . . . it consists in actualizing the universal, and giving it spiritual vitality [*begeisten*], by the process of breaking down and superseding fixed and determinate thoughts." G.W.F. Hegel, *The Phenomenology of Mind*, trans. J. B. Baillie (New York: Harper Torchbooks, 1967), 94.

51. On this metonymy, cf. Rashi, *ad loc., Exod.,* 21:6.

52. That distance and waiting are given every day follows as a theological deduction from "the whole of revelation passes under [*tritt unter*] the great today" (7/2:115).

53. *Wesen/west,* familiar from Heidegger, seems here to connote principally the substantivization of the real as opposed to its active presencing. It is the *topos* of philosophical withdrawal from life into the unreality of questioning (1:31–32; 6:597–98).

54. "On the Uses and Disadvantages of History for Life," section 10, in *Untimely Meditations.*

55. Cf. Max Stirner, *Der Einzige und sein Eigentum* (Leipzig: Philipp Reclam, 1893), 104. Rosenzweig alludes to the latter in (7/1:14); see further (10.645).

56. "Here is the I. The singular human I. Yet wholly receptive, yet only disposed (*aufgetan*), yet empty, without content, without essence, pure readiness . . ." (7/2:113).

57. Friedrich Nietzsche, *On the Genealogy of Morals,* 2. 12.

58.

The most appropriate comparison is here offered by disease, which is the true counterpart of evil and sin, as it constitutes that disorder which entered nature through a misuse of freedom. Disease of the whole organism can never exist without the hidden forces of the depths being unloosed; it occurs when the irritable principle which ought to rule as the innermost tie of forces in the quiet deep, activates itself, or when Archaos is provoked to desert his quiet residence at the center of things and steps forth into the surroundings. So, on the other hand, all radical cure consists in the reestablishment of the relation of the periphery to the center [*der Peripherie zum Centro*], and the transition from disease to health can really take place through its opposite, that is through the restoration of separate and individual life to the inner light of the being, whence there recurs the division (crisis).

Of Human Freedom, 41–42.

59. Leo Strauss, "An Introduction to Heideggerian Existentialism," in *The Rebirth of Classical Political Rationalism: An Introduction to the Thought of Leo Strauss,* ed. Thomas L. Pangle (Chicago: Univ. of Chicago Press, 1989), 28.

Index

Abraham (patriarch), 55
Academy for the Science of
    Judaism, 28, 171–72
Adam (first man), 54, 55, 90
Aesthetics. *See* Art
Agudat Israel, 183n. 11
American scholars, 2, 8, 38
Apollonian culture, 78, 79
Apologetics, 23
Archaos (mythological fig-
    ure), 212n. 57
Aristotle, 7, 90, 208n. 42
Art, 16, 117, 118, 129; avail-
    ability of, 29; interest in,
    26; originary life and, 155;
    religion and, 54; sociology
    of, 95; *Star of Redemption*
    on, 70
Artists, 89
Asian antiquity, 116

Asian religions. *See* Eastern
    religions
Atheism, 107
Athens-Jerusalem question,
    204n. 33
Attic tragedy, 79

Baroque science, 96
Barth, Karl, 178n. 3
"Beeline" theory, 27–28
Belief. *See* Faith
Berdyaev, Nicholas, 178n. 3
Berlin University, 181n. 11
Bible, 28; American scholars
    and, 38; human speech
    and, 36; Jewish explana-
    tion of, 131; narration in,
    18, 201–2n. 26; translation
    of, 8; uniqueness of, 59;